The Natural History of the Somerset Level. 1972 under the title *Sedgemoor; its History* has since come to be regarded as amongst twentieth-century books on English nat a revised fully illustrated edition has long b ue. The change of title reflects the increased attention being given to the Somerset Levels – the name by which they are now generally known.

Bernard Storer is one of the most distinguished of contemporary naturalists and few men or women could be better qualified to be the author of *The Natural History of the Somerset Levels*. He is on the Council of the Somerset Trust for Nature Conservation and is President of the Mid-Somerset Naturalists. He lives on the Levels at Westonzoyland and is well-known for his lectures on their natural history.

Overleaf: *A view from Red Hill showing the flat valley floor with its rectangular fields divided by ditches.*

The Natural History of the Somerset Levels

Bernard Storer

Dovecote Press

First published in 1972
Revised illustrated edition first published in 1985 by
The Dovecote Press Ltd
Stanbridge, Wimborne, Dorset

Revised and reprinted 1987
Reprinted 1990

ISBN 0 9461 59 28 9

Cover design by Humphrey Stone
Printed and bound by Biddles Ltd, Guildford and King's Lynn

Contents

Foreword

'The house in Westonzoyland may be suitable.' I was told this by the estate agent and that same evening I went out to Sedgemoor. As the bus took me clear of Bridgwater and on through the rich green pastures, where there are no hedges but only willow-lined irrigation ditches, I realised that here was something very different from the northern moors where I had grown up. That was in 1958 and even on that first visit I felt something of the atmosphere of this part of the South West.

The house was suitable and before very long I had moved in and started exploring. The land around Westonzoyland is flat, very flat, and one can see over the pastures for miles, up to the dark line of hills marking the boundary of the moorland. One's first impression is that one can walk unhindered, in any direction. However, the lines of willows provide a warning to anyone wishing to prove that the shortest distance between two points is a straight line. One square mile of this flat moorland contains 20 miles of ditches. Since most of these are too wide to jump (I speak from experience), and few of them are bridged, it is safe to say that the distance from A to B is about four times as far as one thinks; and then double that.

A casual stroll in any direction soon shows that these waterways fall into three groups. The largest, about 80ft wide, are called drains, eg King's Sedgemoor Drain. Next in size are the 10–20ft rhynes or rhines (pronounced reens). The narrowest, but by far the most numerous, are the ditches. These may appear to be only 3–4ft across, but are very deceptive because of overhanging bankside vegetation. The actual width can be considerably more, depending on the time of the year, weather conditions, and when they were last cleaned out.

In later chapters the various factors which affect these ditches are dealt with in detail. During heavy rainfall they collect the water from the land and, by passing it through the rhynes to the drains and out to sea, act as drainage ditches. In the dry season the water is penned up in the ditches and their function is reversed as the water goes from them into the pastureland. Up to the beginning of the nineteenth century, Sedgemoor—alternatively known as the Somerset Levels—was mostly neglected; it was low lying and extensively flooded in winter. The land was marshy, with stretches of open water. Since that time, modern drainage

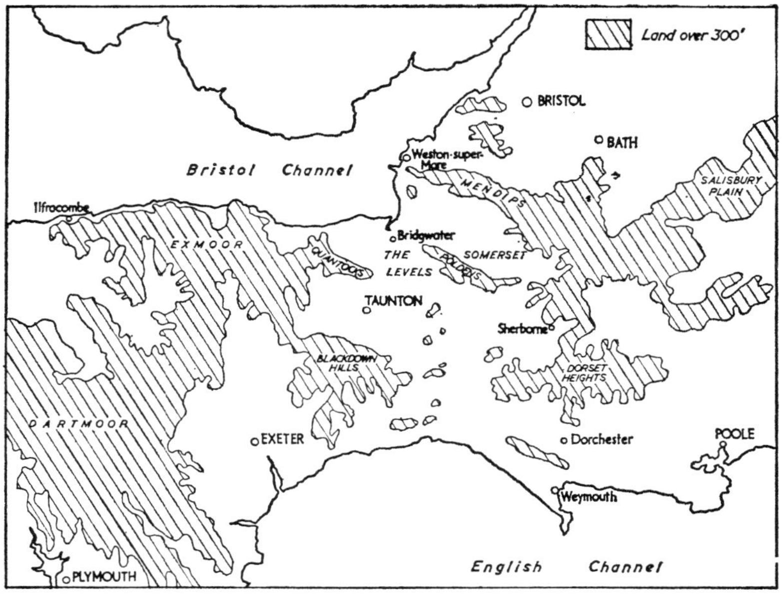

South-west England showing the position of the Somerset Levels.

systems have evolved. To the naturalist, this means that, both in their natural state and since the introduction of man-made ditches, these moors have provided an aquatic and marshy habitat for the plants and animal life which have, in historic times at least, always existed on the Levels. These are the true natives, the oldest inhabitants. But the modern drainage conditions are, at the same time, making it impossible for some of these plants and animals to survive, as their marshy habitat is rapidly ceasing to exist.

It was this thought which first spurred me to find out how many of these old inhabitants were still managing to survive. This led to considering other aspects of the area and what started as a tour of inspection grew into a deep and, in some cases I hope, lasting affection.

This book then is about Sedgemoor, its people and its natural history. In particular it is about the old Sedgemoor, a way of life and living which is fast disappearing.

It is also written with three objects in mind; to record the state of affairs at the time of writing; to encourage the care and protection of the old flora and fauna; and to persuade those who do not know the Somerset Levels to come and be introduced to them. If I succeed in one of these aims I shall be pleased; if I succeed in all three, what more can I ask?

I

Introduction to the Somerset Levels

On the Ordnance Survey Maps of Somerset there is no single place-name 'Sedgemoor'; instead there are large numbers of 'moors'. Some, like King's Sedgemoor, may cover several square miles while others are measured only in acres. The larger moors are usually subdivided and so the site of the Battle of Sedgemoor is shown as Lang Moor, part of King's Sedgemoor. Few of these names are used locally; usually the area is called after the nearest town or village, thus Mark Moor is the land around Mark, and Draycott Moor is the land around Draycott. Alternatively the fields are named after their owners: Jack Smith's field is an adequate description in a stable rural community.

Ditches are sometimes called 'wet fences'. The gate-posts not only mark an entry into each field but also a bridge over the ditch. The access ways are called droves.

To avoid confusion over nomenclature, the whole area has been called Sedgemoor or the Somerset Levels, and it is that part of Somerset to the south-west of the Mendip Hills which lies at or near sea level. Two small areas of equally low-lying ground around Gordano and Kingston Seymour, known as Gordano and Kingston Levels, have been excluded, since they are isolated from the remainder of the region.

To many people, moors are areas of high ground, usually covered with heather and bilberry. The Oxford dictionary defines them as 'areas of waste ground, especially if covered in heather'. On Sedgemoor, the emphasis is on the first part of the definition, the waste ground. Until fairly recently, most of this land was flooded in winter, and in summer covered in the rushes and sedges which give it its name. There were few houses on it and very few trackways across it. During the drier periods, cattle, geese and pigs were pastured on this very rough grazing. Through most of its history, Sedgemoor has been waste or wild land and in this sense 'moor' is not a misnomer.

The main Levels cover more than 200 square miles and lie roughly within the area bounded by the Bristol Channel, the Mendips, south through Glastonbury towards Yeovil, west to Taunton and finally along the eastern edge of the Quantocks back to the Bristol Channel coast (see map, p10). From Brean Down, the coast is composed of sand dunes, as at Berrow; an artificial promenade, as at Burnham; and a complex system of mud flats, shingle ridges and sea walls which continues up to the seaward

Detailed map of the Somerset Levels.

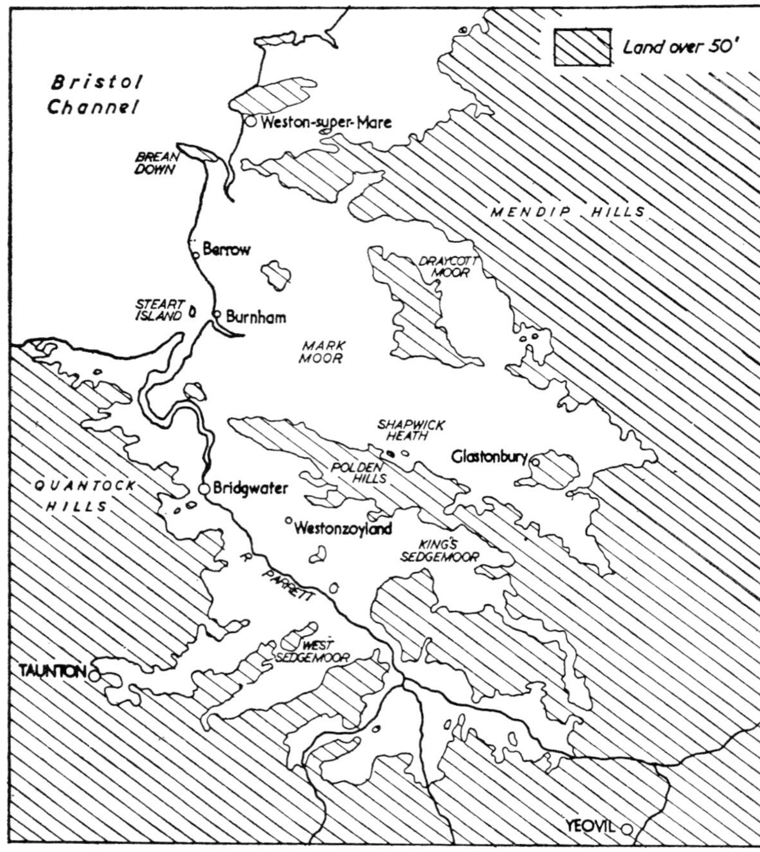

edge of the Quantocks. This coastal belt has also been excluded, except in so far as its distinctive flora and fauna affect the inland life. The large remaining inner basin is cut into two sections by the Polden Hills. These run roughly east–west with Mark Moor, Draycott Moor and Shapwick Heath to the north and King's Sedgemoor and the moors drained by the River Parrett to the south.

Scenically this area does not look very attractive. The land is flat and at first sight seems to be uniformly covered with grass which serves as permanent pasture. The absence of hedges emphasises the apparently ridiculous situation of a gate isolated in the middle of a field. However, if one leaves the main road and walks over these fields then the individuality of the area becomes apparent. The fields are bounded by ditches, and the isolated gate marks a bridge connecting two adjacent fields. 'Wet-land' is a word which has now been coined to cover areas such as marsh, fen and bog.

Over much of England these are fast disappearing; though agriculturally they are usually of poor quality, often they are drained or raised for use as building land. In many ways the Somerset Levels are not wet-lands since the fields now carry permanent pasture and are slightly above the water table.

These flat levels were formed when a landscape was submerged

and the valleys became filled with deposited material. The bottom of these drowned valleys extends 90ft or more beneath the present sea level. Borings indicate that they are filled to approximately the height of the present sea level by a soft blue clay or alluvial silt interspersed with thin layers of peat and gravel. Since the actual height of the sea is a variable factor, some parts of Sedgemoor are below the level of the water in the Bristol Channel. This would suggest marine deposition, but animal and plant remains suggest that the soil was formed under brackish conditions and that the end of the submergence probably occurred about eight thousand years ago. Sphagnum bogs developed over large areas of this water-logged clay and are still to be seen between the Polden Hills and the high ground around Wedmore. Further marine flooding in the late Romano-British period (AD 300–400) brought another deposition of clay. This clay deposit, like the earlier one, was brackish or estuarine in origin and extended well up the valleys of the Rivers Parrett and Axe.

Although the times of deposition vary, the general pattern over

The fields in the foreground are on the lower slopes of the hill. These are usually given over to mixed farming. The central area shows the pastures of Aller Moor.

the Levels is that of a many-layered sandwich. Deposits of clay or silt alternate with organic layers which are the remains of the earlier peat deposits; this general pattern is interrupted in a few places, mostly south of the Poldens, where raised beach deposits (Burtle Beds) break through to the surface and provide a sand-pebble subsoil. These deposits make the ground slightly higher than the surrounding Levels. Villages, such as Westonzoyland, are sited on these raised beach deposits, or on the slopes of the surrounding hills. Immediately around the village each farmer owned, or rented a strip of land. During the winter, when the low-lying fields were flooded, the livestock was brought on to this higher ground for safety. In the spring when the flood waters drained away and the land became firmer, the animals were put out to graze on the Levels. Arable farming was, and still is, exceptional. Winter flooding is now almost eliminated, but the ground remains wet and cold well into the spring. Even with modern machinery it is sometimes difficult, and usually uneconomical, to work the land in winter. Machinery becomes bogged down and much plant growth is retarded.

A number of specialised industries grew up in the district. On West Sedgemoor, a substantial area has long been devoted to withy growing and, until very recently, teasels were grown commercially near Taunton. Around Shapwick a thriving peat industry is rapidly expanding with the boom in horticulture. The blue clay has given rise to a number of brick works around Bridgwater. Some of the gravel deposits are also being worked commercially. Today the complex of waterways is being used more and more for angling and boating, and the now little-used Taunton–Bridgwater canal may also be developed for recreational purposes.

The flat fields of the Levels with the villages on the slightly higher ground above the old flood level.

2

The Old Pattern

The origin of the Levels and the early attempts to drain them

One of the most striking things about Sedgemoor is its individuality: an intangible something which distinguishes it from other parts of the country. In some ways it resembles the flat landscapes of Lincolnshire, but it is more wooded and has a low skyline of hills: the Poldens, the Quantocks and the Mendips. The fields are smaller than in East Anglia and there is far less large-scale arable farming. Because the prevailing wind is a south-westerly one, the climate is generally warm and wet, encouraging the growth of the large number of rushes, sedges and other plants associated with 'wild' places. On an autumn evening with the mist swirling and obscuring the skyline, the heads of apparently disembodied cattle appearing above the ground haze and a few wild-bird calls, Sedgemoor resembles the opening scene in any horror film; yet on a fine summer afternoon it is an ideal place for a picnic. Peace, quiet, a sense of space and of 'oldness' are the feelings which it engenders.

Yet Sedgemoor has obviously changed. The place one sees now is not what prehistoric man would have seen. However, there is very little written evidence to show what the old Sedgemoor looked like. It is only in the middle of this century that it has been possible to discover much about it. This has been due to the development of the technique of pollen grain analysis. Instead of being the fragile structures that one imagines, the grains are now known to be remarkably tough, each species of plant having pollen grains marked or shaped in a distinctive way. Therefore, if the pollen grains are identified from the various depths of the soil, the type of vegetation that was present can be established. Archaeological finds and radio-carbon datings enable a time scale to be put to the sequence. With knowledge of the climatic conditions, soil factors and so on, which are necessary for the particular types of plant growth, it can be deduced what Sedgemoor looked like at various stages in its past. Professor Godwin, who has worked on Shapwick Heath, has been able to show the history of its flora in great detail. From his work the history of most of the area can be reconstructed.

A newly cleaned ditch; the debris can be seen heaped on the right hand bank. The surface has already been colonised by such floating aquatics as Duckweed.

The formation of the Levels

The first flooding

About 6,000 BC the valleys which then existed between the Mendips and the Quantocks were flooded by the sea. This rise in sea level was probably due to the regression and melting of the polar ice. (The sea level in 8,000 BC was certainly more than 100ft below its present level and possibly very much lower.) Because of this marine flooding a large amount of blue-grey clay and silt was deposited, bringing the land in the bottom of the valleys up to approximately its present level. A minor change in the land-sea level followed and the mud began to dry out.

The succession or colonisation process

As these mud flats dried out they were colonised first by reeds (*Phragmites communis*); then this reed-swamp, in turn, was usually invaded by Saw Sedge (*Cladium mariscus*) and by the true sedges (*Carex* spp).

In the reed-beds and ditches existing today can be seen this same succession or sequence whereby one plant type replaces another (see diagrams pp.16,17). Nowadays the starting-point is the open water in a newly cleaned ditch; in earlier times, it was the naturally occurring open pool. It is from the evidence provided by the modern ditches that one can reconstruct what happened about six thousand years ago.

The open water pools were 'invaded' in two ways. Plants such as sedges, rushes and reeds, growing in the marshy ground surrounding the pools, increased in bulk; a clump of rushes will more than double its diameter in one year and sedge rhizomes will stretch several feet from the parent plant, producing two dozen or more new stems. In this way the pools became closed in from the sides. At the same time, true aquatic plants would have been carried by water currents and animals into the open water. In the autumn and winter these aquatic plants would have died and their decaying remains sunk to the floor of the pools. If they rotted away completely then any change would be negligible, but in practice they rotted more slowly than new growth developed.

In this way the total bulk of living and decaying plant material increased year by year and the pools became smaller and shallower. Nowadays a ditch becomes completely overgrown in four to six years; presumably the same time scale applied then.

With the destruction of their habitat, aquatic plants cannot survive; they can be said to carry the seeds of their own destruction within themselves.

However, the British climate is never uniform and whilst one pool was being converted into marshland, another would have been forming elsewhere. The rivers meandered through this landscape, and as they overflowed and cut new channels so new pools formed. The ground was so soft that even heavy rain would have been sufficient to gouge out stretches of open water. Thus, when their habitat was destroyed in one area, the aquatic plants did not become extinct, but were washed to other marshy areas.

During the period 4,000–3,000 BC this process went on over Sedgemoor. The whole area, however, was continuing to dry out and the extent of open water was gradually reduced. One can think of it as changing from marshy islands surrounded by water to an area of marsh containing open pools.

During the drying-out process, the organic debris from the marsh plants accumulated and the ground became firmer. It was now able to support carr—small trees, such as willow and alder, which can thrive in these conditions. In turn, their leaves added yet more material to the soil and eventually patches of it became firm enough to support such woodland trees as ash, oak and elm. Since the succession does not normally go beyond this point, this stage is called the climax.

With this change in the flora there was a corresponding change in the fauna. As new habitats formed at the expense of the old ones, there would have been an introduction of new animals, so that woodland types lived side by side with those inhabiting patches of open water.

This then is the process that occurred in the period 4,000–3,000 BC. The soil was rich in minerals and so fen, or eutrophic, conditions existed.

Here, as in the Fens, a division of the region into a coastal clay or silt area and a hinterland of richer, peatier alluvium became evident. This coastal belt of clay is several miles wide and now dotted with brick-pits, notably between Bridgwater and Highbridge. It is this clay which has been dug up and made into the tiles used in so many local buildings.

The ditch has now become invaded. The ditch bank plants have increased and grown inwards. Other plants, rooted in the mud have emerged in the middle of the ditch.

The ditch is now completely overgrown. The original surface plants have been crowded out and water flow through the ditch is very restricted. The ditch is due for re-cleaning.

The movement back to wetter conditions

In the period about 3,000 BC, towards the end of the Atlantic period and the beginning of the Sub-Boreal period (pollen zones VII A and VII B), another climatic change occurred and the rainfall of the area increased. This affected the vegetation in two ways. Firstly, the amount of water present discouraged the growth of trees unadapted to these wetter conditions, and secondly it washed the essential salts from the soil. As a result, a much wetter and poorer soil was produced. In the first stage of these new conditions, which are called oligotrophic, the vegetation was a mixture of Cotton-grass (*Eriophorum* spp), heaths (*Erica* spp) and mosses (chiefly *Sphagnum* spp). The pollen distribution shows a distinct drop in the elm and birch populations, while the peat which formed in this period is a Sphagnum moss peat.

It is now suggested that in this early Sub-Boreal period the decline in the population of elm trees in some parts of England was due to the activities of Neolithic man, as there is good evi-

Diagrams showing the various stages of natural succession, from open water to woodland, in a typical Levels ditch.

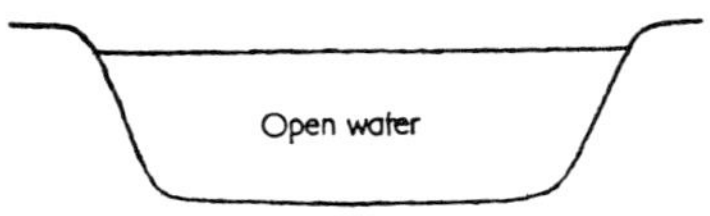

Stage 1
Profile through newly cleaned ditch, an open community

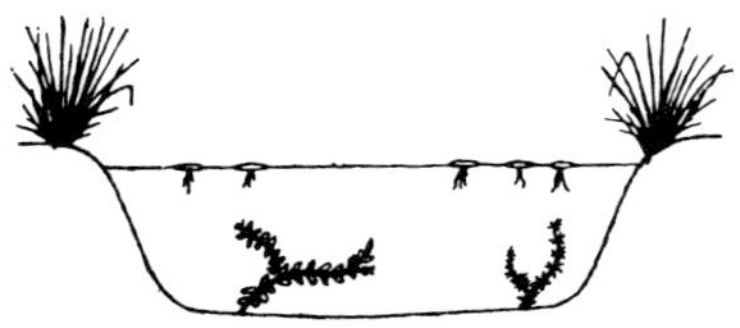

Stage 2
Invasion of the ditch by aquatic plants and by plants from the banks

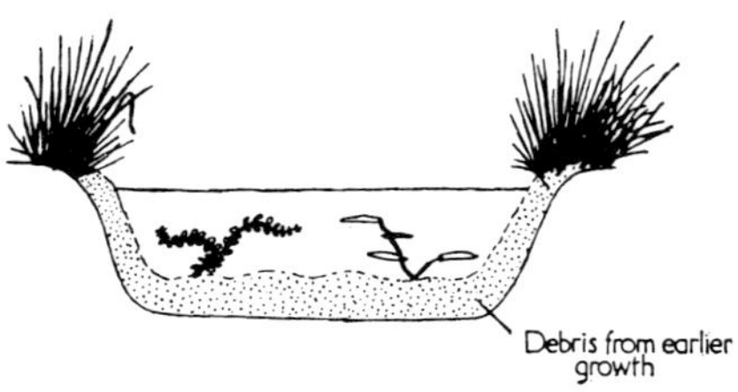

Stage 3
The ditch becomes narrower and shallower

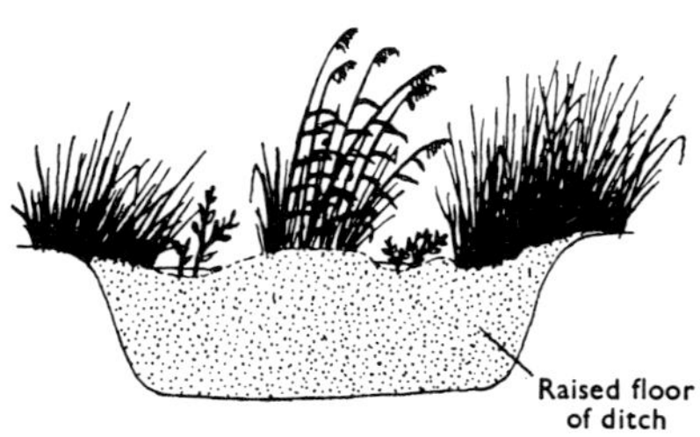

Stage 4
The ditch is almost completely 'filled-in' and very little open water is left for the few remaining aquatic plants

dence that forest clearing was practised about this time. On Sedgemoor, however, it seems unlikely that man was in any way responsible for the decrease in the elms; his burning and felling was usually limited to the drier uplands. The oak-tree population remained relatively unchanged, but the alder and probably the Bog Myrtle populations increased very considerably. It would, therefore, seem far more likely that this vegetational change mirrored a climatic change.

Once these bog, or oligotrophic, conditions arose, the soil changed not only from salt rich to salt poor, but from alkaline to acid. This was partly due to the removal, by leaching out, of the base rich salts such as compounds of calcium, and partly to the increase in carbon dioxide and hence carbonic acid. Providing that the high level of precipitation persisted, then such a bog was capable of growing. In its centre, the dead plant remains exerted a capillary effect and 'sucked up' the water from the underlying water table. Therefore, instead of being superceded by the next stage in the succession, the bog plants kept the ground in a very wet, oligotrophic condition. The centre of such a bog, subjected to high rainfall and unaffected by water-carrying dissolved salts, became self-generating. Shapwick Heath bog continued to grow until about AD 300, when it stopped for some as yet unexplained reason.

Due to the acidic conditions, the rate of decay of the vegetation was even slower than normal and the floor of the bog became raised by the earlier years' debris. In profile, such a bog looked like an inverted saucer, and as the centre became raised so the water table rose to correspond with it and the land remained boggy. In parts of Shapwick Heath today it is rather like walking on a trampoline and a firm stamp on the ground makes the surface ripple for several yards around. It is in these conditions that peat is formed.

These acid conditions discourage nitrifying bacteria which normally help in the breakdown of organic material so that the nitrogen may be reabsorbed and used in protein synthesis. In the absence of these bacteria several species of plants have evolved alternative methods of obtaining their nitrogen and a number of these can be found on the peat moors. Some, such as Sundew, Bladderwort and Butterwort, are insectivorous; others, like Lousewort, Eyebright and Yellow Rattle, are semi-parasitic.

As the centre of the bog became raised, the water flowed outwards towards the edge; in this way the bog tended to grow outwards as well as upwards. On the Levels, however, the following conditions kept the fringes of the bog in balance: The Polden Hills are lias limestone and the Mendips carboniferous limestone; outliers of lias also occur at Meare, Wedmore and Brent Knoll. Water draining from these surrounding hills contained mineral salts and especially calcium salts. Thus immediately

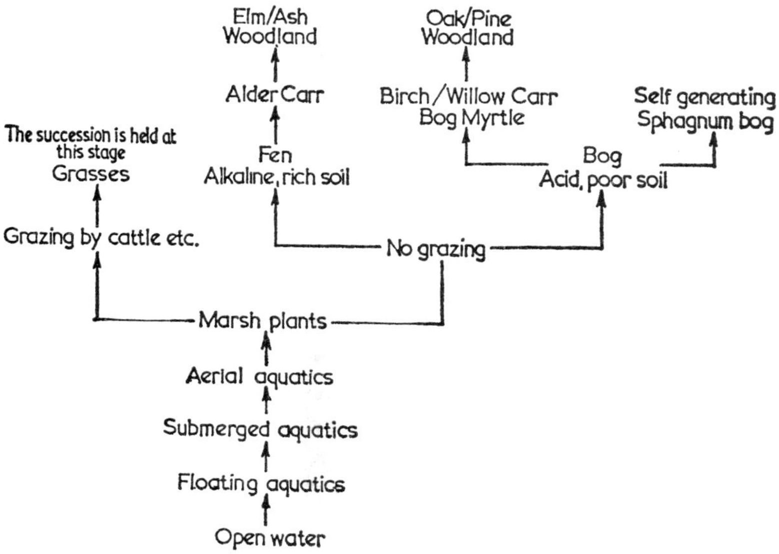

Stage 5
The site of the ditch is filled with marsh plants and young carr is becoming established

around the Levels was a rim where eutrophic conditions pertained. During periods of relatively low rainfall, the salt rich water spread out on to the Levels and eroded the edges of the raised bog. With heavy rainfall, the encroaching salts were quickly leached downwards and the bog extended right up to the slopes of the hills.

Throughout the Sub-Boreal period the Levels were covered by these raised bogs. It would seem, however, that the weather became drier and the growth rate of the bogs slowed down; at the end of the Late Bronze Age growth had almost ceased and a dry bog surface resulted, which was often colonised by Ling or Heather (*Calluna vulgaris*). Below this dry surface, which lasted until about 500 BC, the peat is dark and highly humified and shows little in the way of texture.

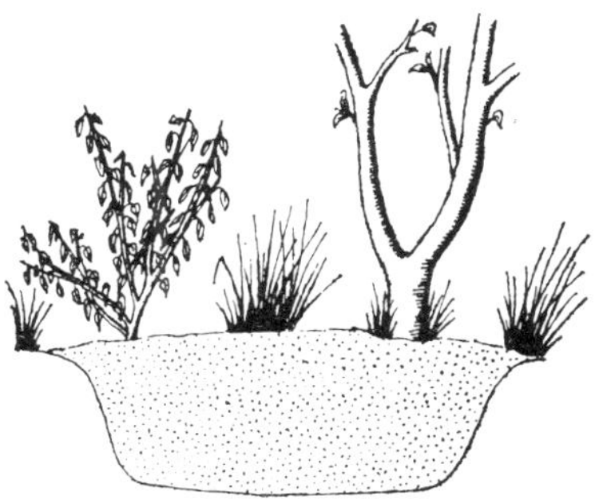

Stage 6
The marsh plants are suppressed by the carr and, if grazing is prohibited, a further rise in ground level can occur due to the dead leaves, etc from the overhanging trees.
Finally the alder- birch- willow carr is replaced by true woodland trees. This is the climax stage.

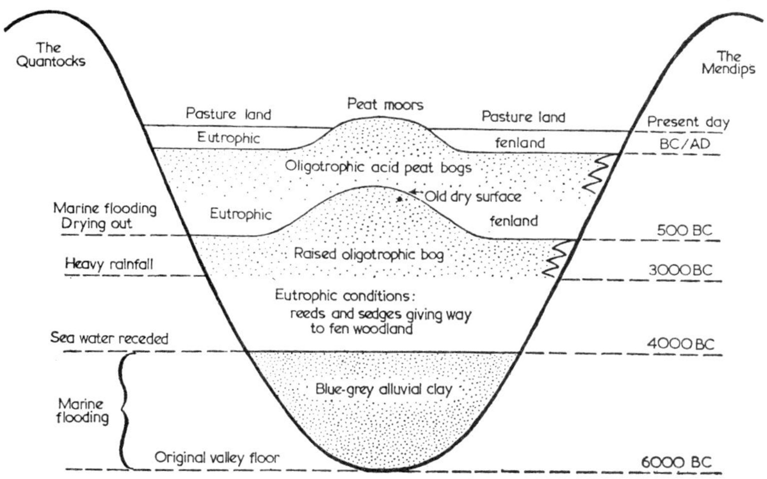

A diagrammatic section through the Levels (not to scale) indicating the evolutionary process from 6,000 BC to the present day.

The influence of early man

The Neolithic and Bronze Age periods

Much of the archaeological evidence of human activity up to this time relates to trackways. The earliest period of road building was Neolithic; a later one occurred during the Bronze Age.

One of the Neolithic trackways, called Bell Track, has been dated by the radio-carbon method at 2890 BC (± 100), which makes it the oldest wooden trackway in the world. The other trackway, Abbots Track, dated from the same period (2850 BC ± 110), was the first to be examined. It was discovered in the early nineteenth century and got its name from its alignment towards Glastonbury. The track was lost to view from about 1890 to 1960, but since 1964 there have been a number of new borings and diggings, and the road can now be traced for about two miles, from Catcott Burtle to Westhay.

Because of its appearance it has been called a corduroy road. Split trunks of alder were laid across the line of the road and, considering the nature of the ground, were perhaps more analogous to the planks of a raft. One can imagine the road in winter almost floating on the wet peat like a pontoon bridge. It also suggests that a sledge type of vehicle might have been used rather than a wheeled one.

The alder planks, and some were true planks in that they were trimmed on both sides, were held in place by birch pegs at the sides. It seems likely that thin birches were then woven along to hold the cross bars to the pegs. Considering the work involved—it has been estimated that 50,000 pegs were needed—Abbots Track must have been a fairly important road. Yet it is difficult to visualise where it is going to. It would seem likely that any north–south track, from the Mendips to the Poldens, would use Westhay, which is a little higher than the surrounding moor. But why go north–west from Westhay? The road points to what is now Highbridge. Allowing for movement of the coastline, was there some sort of port in that area? It is even possible that at an earlier date, when the coastline was further inland than it is now, an organised system of waterways was in use and the stones for Stonehenge were brought by water over much of the present Sedgemoor. Alternatively, the track could have led to the camps at Brent Knoll and Pawlett.

The second track, Bell Track, has been excavated at the Westhay end of Abbots Track. In this case the transverse planks were of ash; a mattress of hazel twigs about 1ft thick was put down on top and held in place by birch pegs. A wooden hermaphrodite figurine, now called a 'corn dolly', was found near this trackway within the last decade.

Tracks built in the later period, also wooden, were probably put down about 700–600 BC. Late Bronze Age artifacts, as well as more recent ones, have been found in association with these

tracks. Occasionally one is lucky enough to see part of a trackway exposed when the peat is being worked.

About 500 BC another change affected the Levels and much of the area was again flooded, this time probably by sea water. The raised bog on Shapwick Heath was high enough by this time to be only partly affected by the flooding. The profile of the peat again reflects the change of conditions. Above the old dark brown humified peat there is often a thin line marking the detritus mud brought in by the flooding and above this there appears lighter brown fibrous new peat. This abrupt change, a recurrence surface, is sometimes called the Grenz Horizont.

The flood water was rich in calcium, which brought about a return to eutrophic conditions over most of the Levels: the area once more moved towards fen woodland.

Two photographs showing a team of archaeologists excavating an ancient trackway. The planks are used to keep their own weight off the trackway itself. Much of the recovery depends on very careful and painstaking work. The bottom illustration shows the exposed trackway.

The lake villages

Between Meare and Glastonbury there was a large pool or lake. It was about five miles in circumference by the sixteenth century and persisted until fairly recently. Excavations in the area during the last eighty years revealed a picture of the Meare and Glastonbury 'lake villages'. The latest discoveries at Meare indicate that the first phase of occupation occurred when the 'shore'—itself a bog surface—was relatively dry and firm. A number of small round

A reconstruction, from the Castle Museum Taunton, showing the features of a "Lake Village" house.

This boat was dug out from the peat near Shapwick in 1916 and is now in the Castle Museum, Taunton. Dating techniques show it to be about 2,250 years old. A similar boat can be seen in the Glastonbury Tribunal Museum.

houses were built on a clay and brushwood base about the third century BC. The first interpretation of these finds was that the houses were supported over the water on stilts; this led to the name 'lake village'. More recent work, however, suggests that the peat was dry enough to support a more conventional Iron Age settlement. It now seems likely that the original settlement was on the slightly higher ground of the Meare-Westhay area, the 'lake villages' being an extension of this settlement. Although relatively few finds can be definitely assigned to this phase, they give some idea of the life of the people. Axe marks show that the carpentry was good. Remains of four boats so far found display the same ability. One is a 17ft dugout canoe, which can be seen along with other objects from the site in the Glastonbury Museum. The second boat is about the same size, but its shape is nearer to that of the present-day punt. A third boat was found in the peat, but was broken up and used as fuel. A section of a fourth boat discovered near Glastonbury indicates that the original was about 40ft long.

Excavations show that there was a settled community, with the settlement at the Meare end of the lake pre-dating the Glastonbury one. Wheat, barley, peas and beans were grown and the remains of animals indicate that herds and flocks were maintained.

Horses, sheep and goats, as well as dogs and cats, were almost certainly domesticated, while deer, beaver, otter and pine marten were hunted. It is not known whether pigs (or boars) and swans were domesticated. Certainly the presence of pine marten and beaver as well as pelican and sea eagles indicates both woodland and water—doubtless with areas of open peat bog in between.

Weaving was practised on a sizeable scale, and the community either supported craftsmen or could afford to import such luxuries as glass beads and bronze brooches, as well as bronze and iron tools.

Sometime in the second century BC the site was abandoned. Although there is no direct evidence, it seems likely that the site became too wet and the people moved back to the main settlement at Meare. The 'lake village' became a rubbish dump and it is from this material that the majority of the finds have been recovered; later, hundreds of tons of clay were tipped on the rubbish dump. Scraps of bronze trinkets and decorated pottery were found scattered over these clay mounds. Dated to the first century BC, these finds indicated that the people were still living on the Meare 'island' rather than on the site itself.

During that century there is clear evidence of flooding and it was not until after the third century AD that there is any indication that the site was reoccupied. These later finds, Roman coins and pottery, unfortunately tell us little about the people who lived there during that period.

In 1968 a series of excavations carried out in Westonzoyland produced a number of Late Pre-Roman Iron Age finds. Flints suggested a very early occupation, but the recovered pottery puts the bulk of the finds in the period just before and during the Roman occupation. An excavated site at Alstone, near West Huntspill, shows that the raised ground of the Burtle Bed sands was occupied during the same period. At Alstone the sand is covered by clay deposited near the end of the fourth century AD, thus putting a terminal date to the occupation. Since the Westonzoyland site is on slightly higher ground it may well be that it has been in continual use.

The occupation of these small islands of Burtle Bed sands raises two queries. Firstly, although the moor may have been dry enough at times for normal access, it seems more likely that these sites were linked by trackways, still awaiting discovery. The second and more fundamental question is why they were occupied. Perhaps an expanding population had to choose between clearing the forest and occupying these inhospitable marsh islands, where the light scrub could be more easily cleared for crop-planting.

The Roman occupation

The rest of the Levels reverted to oligotrophic bog until about AD 250. Once again the land/sea levels changed and the area was flooded with sea water. This brought in a deposit of brown clay, often called 'Roman clay', which overlies the old blue-grey clay. Despite local legend, there is no evidence of a Roman sea wall. The fact that this clay was found in depth along the coastal strip, when clay was being dug out for tile and brick making, probably gave rise to the story. The 'Roman clay' extends up to Langport; even as far inland as this it is nearly 3ft thick. It has been calculated that something like 1,000 million tons of clay were laid down during this period of flooding!

A Roman villa, below the present sea level, near Yatton, and a stone inscription on the Welsh coast have been adduced to support the theory that the Romans built the first sea walls. It now seems likely, however, that when the villa was built it was above the high-tide level of the period; retaining sea walls would not have been necessary. The link between possible work on the Welsh coast and an assumption that walls were built on the Somerset coast is too tenuous by itself. Without more evidence the Romans cannot be credited with being the first to attempt to control the flooding.

Inland there is definite evidence about the Roman occupation of Sedgemoor. When drainage work was being carried out at Highbridge at the beginning of the nineteenth century, Roman remains, including coin moulds, were found. Further evidence of Roman occupation appeared in the 1940s when Huntspill Cut was being dug. Quite recently, Miles, excavating a brick pit at Highbridge, discovered a Roman ground surface dating to the middle of the second century; and in 1960 Nash and Smith recovered evidence of Roman building in the same area.

Further inland, north of the Poldens, clay coin moulds provide evidence of occupation during the early part of the third century. Long before this, in AD 49, the Romans were mining lead in the Mendips. Even before the occupation, it is likely that they traded for Mendip lead; it is even possible that earlier still the Phoenicians were involved in this trade. In general, the Roman occupation and settlement shows that they chose the higher agricultural areas and avoided the low-lying marshland. The positions of Roman villas are sited along their road from Ilchester to Somerton, then north and west along the Polden Hills. Whether or not Greylake fosse, part of the A361, was a Roman road crossing Sedgemoor is a point for discussion. Ilchester itself was a Roman town or at least a posting station along the Fosse Way. Its relevance to Sedgemoor lies in its Roman wharves, indicating that the River Parrett and its tributary, the River Ivel (Yeo), were navigable in those days.

Sedgemoor and flooding in historical times

After this major flooding of AD 250, there is little evidence that man tried to control the environment until the medieval monasteries became involved. What little is known of the area during King Alfred's reign suggests that it was wild and marshy with very few trackways across it. Athelney, where according to legend he burnt the cakes, is often referred to as the *isle* of Athelney, implying that the surrounding Sedgemoor was either under water or very marshy indeed. It was from here that Alfred moved out to defeat the Danes in 878 at Edington. A large body of opinion puts the site of the battle at Edington in Wiltshire but there is an argument for suggesting that it was fought at Edington on the Poldens. This would perhaps explain why negotiation with the Danes took place at Wedmore.

The Alfred Jewel. This jewel of gold and enamel was found near Athelney in 1693. It was, perhaps, the top of a staff and it bears the Saxon inscription 'Alfred had me made'. The original is in the Bodleian Museum.

The flooding–recolonisation cycle

Why did Sedgemoor remain in this fenny, marshy state until about two hundred years ago? If man did not interfere, why did the natural succession not lead to a woodland climax? Why was the area not part of the forest land which covered much of England? When Moss was surveying the vegetation of Somerset at the beginning of this century he stated, about the Levels, 'The land was primitively treeless. Not a single example of natural woodland occurs and even plantations are uncommon.' Later he reinforces this with the comment 'There are no . . . indigenous trees or shrubs. There can be no doubt that the Levels were primitively treeless.' Woodland did occur in the earlier eutrophic fens, as is now known, but Moss was right when he said that there was no evidence of mature woodland on the present surface of the Levels. The fact that the normal vegetational succession did not take place suggests that the land-water levels remained in the same relative positions. Minor influences could have been the removal of peat for fuel, and wind erosion over the dried peat surface would also have helped to lower the land surface to counteract the successional build-up. However, these factors only apply to small areas and are not adequate to explain the whole problem.

It seems probable, therefore, that continual flooding is the predominant reason for Sedgemoor existing as it does now.

Four types of flooding can be distinguished. Firstly, there were the major, long-lasting inundations due to climatic changes or land–sea level shifts whose chief effect was to deposit alluvial silts and clays over Sedgemoor.

Secondly, there have been large-scale marine floods, often following a break in the sea wall.

The Bristol Channel has the second highest tide range in the world. The tides are slightly higher on the Welsh side of the Channel and at Monmouth they average 38ft and occasionally reach 50ft. Moss quotes Kelly's Directory as recording a rise of 70ft on one occasion. On the Somerset side, a tide of 44ft has been recorded at Bridgwater bridge. This means that those parts of the Levels which are 20ft above sea level are roughly at the

Flooding around Langport. The town itself is on the slightly higher ground.

same level as the sea water when it is high tide in the Channel. Large areas of the Levels are about 20ft above sea level and in many regions they are considerably below this height. Moss gives us the following table:

	Height above sea level
Aller Moor	17ft
West of King's Sedgemoor	14ft
Puriton Level	17ft
Weston Level (near Moorland)	12ft
Catcott Heath	10ft
North of Westhay	9ft

These figures emphasise that at high tide the land would be flooded by sea water. In the early stages, the Levels were probably rather like an enormous mud beach, exposed at low tide and covered by the sea when the tide rose. In places like Westonzoyland, sandbanks formed and even now there is only a thin crust of soil over the underlying sand. When, in 1960, the main drains were laid through the village, the excavators dug out almost pure sand. Until fairly recently, some local builders simply dug a hole on the site and used the sand which was uncovered. About two thousand years ago these higher 'islands' were probably rather like Steart Island is today, accessible at low tide but cut off during the high tides.

It is likely that a sea wall was created naturally. When fresh water, carrying suspended, fine mud particles, is mixed with sea water, the particles flocculate and 'settle out'. This would have happened when fresh water draining off the Levels met the incoming sea water. Some of this 'settling out' would have helped to raise the land level all over the area, but most of it would have occurred along the 'average' coast line, about mid-tide level. Once this process starts, the sea water is held for longer periods at this point and more deposition goes on in this particular area. In this way the land level becomes higher and more effective, and so the area where the fresh and salt water meet becomes more restricted, until eventually a natural sea wall builds up.

Various artificial devices are used to reinforce a sea wall so that marine flooding is reduced or prevented. Nowadays the sea defences, controlled by the Somerset River Authority, prove completely effective. In the past, the efforts of authorities responsible for maintaining the walls were not always so successful. A woodcut of about 1607 illustrates one such occasion, when a very unconcerned babe is shown floating in its crib past the top of what is probably Chedzoy church tower.

In 1607 the coast defences gave way near Burnham and resulted in a hundred square miles of land being flooded. Thirty villages were submerged and sixty-five people from the Uphill, Brean and Huntspill area lost their lives. In 1811 floods reached Glastonbury and again most of Sedgemoor was under water.

As these extensive marine floods receded, much of the soil and

A woodcut commemorating the floods of 1607.

organic debris built up by the succession was carried away. The major floods were serious enough to be recorded, but many minor breakthroughs must also have occurred.

The third type of flooding is the 'normal' winter flooding.

The Levels are surrounded by hills and drained by several rivers. Up to 1930 it was normal for the winter precipitation to result in more water entering the Levels than could get away. The sea walls controlled the exit as well as the entrance of flood water, and swollen rivers could not get rid of it fast enough. The water had to be either pumped away or left until the spring when the rivers could carry it away. The Levels were divided into smaller areas by earth flood banks to control this winter flooding. If no precautions were taken, a swollen river could burst its banks almost anywhere and the resulting flood water might have endangered Bridgwater and other populated localities. To relieve the pressure in the rivers, excess water was allowed to spill over into relatively 'safe' areas, such as Aller Moor, where the damage would be minimal. Indeed, some farmers welcomed this, as the silt helped to enrich the soil and, at the same time, farmland pests, such as field-mice and voles, were greatly reduced. This type of flooding also resulted in much newly formed soil being washed away. Hann estimated that the water of the Bristol Channel contained 0·557 grammes of supended material per litre, and recent surveys show that on incoming tides the River Parrett holds 1·8 grammes per litre of suspended particles. On Hann's figure of just over half a gramme per litre he estimated that the water of the Bristol Channel contains 700,000 tons of suspended material.

Not only was the soil lost but that which remained was com-

Withies (osiers) have been utilised through much of the history of the Levels. Here the cut withies are being transported by boat. There is more detail about withies in the chapter dealing with local industries.

pacted down by the weight of water standing on it. It is likely that the older organic layers incorporated in the alluvium were especially affected by this compression and thereby the effect of the flood water in lowering the land level was enhanced.

Lastly, there are the summer flash floods which are usually the result of exceptionally heavy rain and have little effect on the overall pattern.

Thus it would seem likely that a cycle was set up. Very low lying areas below the water table were stretches of open water. Natural succession took place, the soil level gradually rose, becoming very marshy until it reached carr or even fen woodland. Somewhere along this sequence, flooding would occur, much of the built-up ground would be washed away and the remainder compacted by the weight of the flood water. So, once again, the area would have reverted to an open aquatic habitat. It is also likely that areas would be affected at different times, the course of the drainage rivers would change and patches of open water and patches at various stages of succession would exist side by side. In this way there would have been suitable habitats for a wide range of plants and animals.

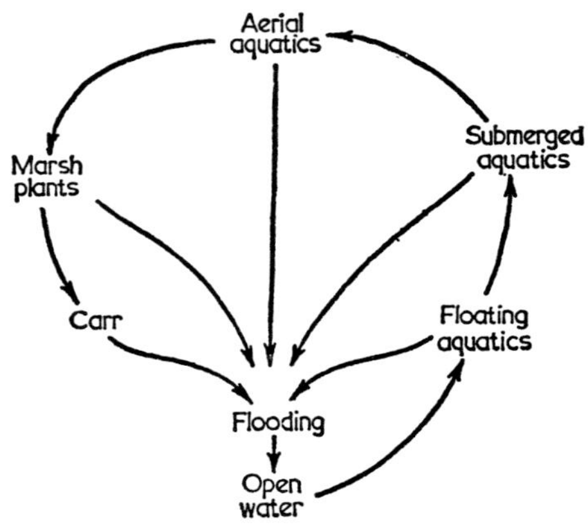

The natural cycle of flooding and succession.

Although this flooding cycle has affected most of Sedgemoor for the last two thousand years, most of the Shapwick Heath area has been relatively uninvolved, because of its raised centre. Around the edges of the Heath are a compact series of habitats showing all the stages in the succession. Standing there, it is easy to visualise what most of Sedgemoor looked like in Romano-British times. Moving to the centre of the Heath, one passes through a carr woodland belt to mature trees of beech and oak, and such associated woodland plants as honeysuckle. Taking the pattern even further, there is the White Admiral butterfly whose caterpillars feed on the honeysuckle. This typical woodland butterfly can be seen here side by side with the dragonfly.

Widespread flooding in 1963.

The early attempts to utilise and drain the Levels

From the Norman Conquest onwards there is written evidence, though admittedly only scanty, about Sedgemoor and man's attempts to break the natural cycle.

The Saxons assigned parts of the moor to nearby villages or groups of villages. In the drier periods it provided rough grazing for cattle, pigs and geese, and during the winter floods a home for visiting wild fowl. By 1340 there was a swannery near Wedmore. The Domesday Book refers to fifteen fisheries on Sedgemoor. To what extent these fish ponds were man-made is not clear; it is likely that they ranged from cleared natural pools to artificial ponds. Later evidence shows that the waterways too were an important source of fish: eel, salmon, pike, lamprey, flounder, bream and tench are recorded as being taken. In 1337, when the Bishop of Bath and Wells was travelling across Sedgemoor, his party consumed 1,060 eels, besides roach, perch, minnows, salmon, bream and pickerel.

Rushes and reeds from the moor were used in the home and sometimes as dowries. Tithes of reed-beds were often reserved for the local priest; in 1235, 100 bundles of reeds cost about 9d. Osiers were cut for basket making; and for this purpose it seems likely that, in addition to willows of natural growth, some osier beds were planted. Peat provided much of the fuel and transport was largely by water.

By the thirteenth century, the religious houses at Wells and Glastonbury and the abbeys at Muchelney and Athelney were making attempts to improve the undrained areas and even to organise reclamation work. However, these were little more than nibblings around the edge of the Levels; there was no co-ordinated effort to change the character of Sedgemoor. Perhaps the most significant step was the attempt by tenants of the coastal strip to maintain the sea wall.

Inland, some of the drainage schemes were moderately successful, parts of the moor were enclosed and grass grown for hay making.

Eventually specific claims for commoning were established and there was a move towards accepting exclusive rights in a limited area in exchange for more general rights. This meant that areas had to be defined and led to what is still the practice, ie boundary by ditch. This exchange of rights led to a very complex situation; for example, at Thurlemere, near Brent, the moor belonged to the Dean of Wells, yet the Abbot of Glastonbury, the villagers of East Brent, South Brent, Berrow and Lympsham and five lords all had the rights of commoning there.

At this period the land was graded into marsh, mow, pasture and meadow, and one can imagine the arguments that must have raged when land was upgraded and taxed accordingly. Some idea of the general pattern can be gained from Abbot Michael's survey of the Westonzoyland, Middlezoy and Othery area in 1238. This was described as the richest of the Abbot's holdings on the Levels proper (as distinct from land bordering them). The holding of land in the three villages was 1,275 acres, split into 112 holdings held at an average of 4d per acre. On the surrounding moor were 722 acres of meadow shared by 177 holdings, varying in size from half an acre to twenty-four acres, but in most cases averaging three to five acres.

A land dispute at Edington in 1253 could not be settled at the time because 'the tenement of which complaint is made is so covered by water that a view cannot be made'.

The drainage problem then as now is twofold. Firstly, to keep

The Abbots Fish House near Glastonbury. Fish formed a significant part of the mediaeval diet and fish ponds, with their associated buildings – the fore runners of the modern fish farm – were a feature of the life of that period.

out the sea; secondly, the removal of fresh water which collects during the winter.

It seems probable that the monks of Glastonbury tackled the problem by straightening the River Brue and putting in a sluice at Highbridge. They certainly built a sea wall and made the six-mile Pillrow Cut from the River Brue near Catcott to the old course of the River Axe near Biddisham.

Apart from improving the drainage, these cuts, with other smaller ones, became boundary marks, enclosures for cattle, means of transport and a source of fish. Mud from the ditches was added to the fields as fertiliser. So the waterways became of value and tenants rights were established. In general the rights from the larger schemes went to the lords of the land; the duality of rights and obligations of both lords and commoners meant that when the medieval pattern began to wane inefficiency quickly set in. In 1443 the Abbot of Athelney and some of his tenants were summoned for neglecting ditches. There was also a clash of interests between those who saw the waterways as a transport system and wanted free access, and those who saw them as a source of fish and wanted to erect weirs, or as a source of power for the mills.

At about the end of the twelfth century, Richard I gave permission to the Bishop of Wells for a port at Rackley on the River Axe. The river was tidal up to that point and the port was mainly concerned with shipping lead from the Mendip mines. Smaller craft could go upstream to Panborough, from which goods were taken along the higher and firmer ground to Wells.

Further south, at Rooksbridge, near East Brent, the Abbots of Glastonbury had their port on a tidal pill of the old river. The route from the port followed the Pillrow Cut to Mark and then turned south-east to the River Brue below Burtle; from there goods went via Meare Pool to Glastonbury. Considering the

An early photograph showing part of the ruins of Glastonbury Abbey. This was once one of the richest Benedictine houses in Britain. There are links, in folk lore and in history, with Joseph of Arimathea, King Arthur, King Alfred and St Dunstan and the Glastonbury Thorn grows in its grounds. The ruins, now cleaned of ivy, are open to the public.

amount of work that would have been involved, it seems likely that the original Pillrow Cut was a natural waterway, perhaps at some time draining Meare Pool into the River Axe. This would have been straightened and made navigable in the first quarter of the fourteenth century. Some time later the Upper and Lower Brue channels were connected. The records of St John's Church, Glastonbury, show details of the route from Bristol via Rooksbridge and the Pillrow Cut which was used when new church seats were obtained in 1500.

Minor waterways around Meare were used by the abbots for small-scale local traffic, but at the dissolution of the monasteries this whole complex ceased to be maintained and the Pillrow Cut eventually became the Mark Yeo. However, the River Axe continued to be navigable to Rackley and Lower Weare where the river was bridged by the Bridgwater road. At this period its traffic gradually switched from carrying lead outwards to bringing coal inland to Axbridge.

South of the Poldens, the River Parrett carried traffic up to and beyond Langport. The river was tidal almost as far as the town, and it had, and still has, a bore. This is a very small cousin of the Severn bore, but it did help barges to ascend the river. (By Charles I's time, barges of 15–20 tons were in use.) The normal practice seems to have been to use the larger barges as far as possible and then, just up river of Langport, to transfer the goods to smaller barges which continued up towards Ilchester and Muchelney.

Flooding was obviously a danger with a slow meandering river such as the Parrett and, even by Richard I's time, the banks had been built up. This not only reduced flooding, but by penning more water in the river it aided navigation.

During the medieval period, the general pattern was to improve Sedgemoor, prevent flooding, drain the land and utilise the waterways as a means of transport. This progress might have continued, but the state of unrest in the country, culminating in the dissolution of the monasteries, brought all reclamation schemes to a halt and much of the work already done fell into disrepair. No real efforts were made to control the flooding until 1680, when King James laid claim to the soil of the moor and formed the design of improving what is now King's Sedgemoor by a complete drainage system. This was opposed by the owners of adjacent lordships and the scheme fell through.

Sedgemoor became well known five years later when the Monmouth rebellion was crushed just outside Westonzoyland, an episode often quoted as the last battle fought on English soil. Monmouth marched his men from Bridgwater towards Chedzoy and then turned south to Westonzoyland. They were halted at Bussex rhyne and defeated there. Bussex rhyne cannot be reliably traced, but the maps of the period show it as extending in a curve

The memorial to those who fell at the Battle of Sedgemoor. 1985 marks the three hundredth anniversary of the battle.

to the north and west of the village. Since man-made rhynes and ditches were cut in a straight line, the Bussex rhyne was most likely an old river bed, probably of the River Cary or River Parrett.

The battle memorial, erected at the beginning of this century, stands only a few hundred yards from King's Sedgemoor Drain which replaced the original river. The wording obviously presented some difficulty. Technically Monmouth's followers committed treason and could not be lauded in the usual way. Eventually, it was decided to commemorate those who fell 'doing the right as they gave it'—a tactful way out of the difficulty. Westonzoyland church records show that some of the wounded were kept there immediately after the battle. At least three buildings in the area claim that marks of wear on the stonework are 'where the government troops sharpened their swords'. Occasionally relics of the battle are brought up during ditch cleaning.

Once more Sedgemoor passed into obscurity and, by the end of the seventeenth century, the Levels probably looked much as they had done for thousands of years.

3
The New Pattern

In the Brue valley. Locally dug peat being transported by boat.

The first modern attempts to drain the moors; 1770 to the mid-nineteenth century

The early attempts to drain the moor were, by their small scale and unco-ordinated effort, unlikely to make any appreciable difference. At the end of the eighteenth century, Billingsley wrote: 'Here we descend into the marsh or fen lands. This country has been heretofore much neglected, being destitute of gentlemen's houses, probably on account of the stagnant waters and unwholesome air. On these bogs scarce any pasturage at present grows. They are a composition of porous substances, floating on water and imbibing it like a sponge. They are observed to rise with much wet, and sink in dry weather.'

Man had made trackways across the moors and used some of their products, but basically he had adapted to the moors. Now the moors began to be adapted to man's requirements. In modern terms the ecology of the moor was to be changed to suit mass-producing man and he would no longer need to adopt farming methods appropriate to the area. Work on the East Anglian fens had shown that it was possible to drain and control large areas. The enclosure acts and general 'climate of opinion' were other factors which influenced ideas on the draining of Sedgemoor.

Between 1770 and 1833 the moor was enclosed. Each parliamentary act of enclosure contained provisions for draining the area, and enclosure boundaries coincided with drainage boundaries. It is easier to consider the work as it affected different sections of the moor, while bearing in mind that they were being drained more or less simultaneously.

The Brue Valley

Work started in 1770 on the Brue Valley and for the first ten years was carried out on too small a scale. This only resulted in ridding one moorland block of water at the expense of another. In addition, the indirect course of the River Brue meant that there was too little fall, and the clyce (a local name for a sluice) at Highbridge was too small. The Brue Valley Drainage Act was passed in 1801, allowing for the river to be straightened and thus increasing its angle of descent. At the same time, a new clyce at Highbridge with a lower sill allowed more water to escape. Two relief drains, the North Drain and South Drain, were cut but, since their outfall was into the River Brue, they were not very effective. However, the effect of these schemes should not be underestimated. Before the drainage took place, it is recorded that 10,000 sheep rotted in one year in the parish of Mark.

Whilst the drains were being dug, efforts were made to improve the peat area. Clay was dumped on it and also the silt that was scraped out of the rhynes. Controlled flooding, or warping, was encouraged so that the silt in the flood water would settle out and raise the land level. This sharply illustrates the new type of thinking: instead of choosing plants which could grow in the wet acid soil, attempts were being made to change the character of the soil so that other crops could be introduced. In the centre of the peat bogs, a certain amount of tree planting—fir, birch and alder—was carried out. Although this gave brushwood for fuel, presumably the main reason was to encourage a soil build-up, utilising the dead leaves and so on, much as happens in the natural way. The descendants of some of these trees can probably be seen on Shapwick Heath today.

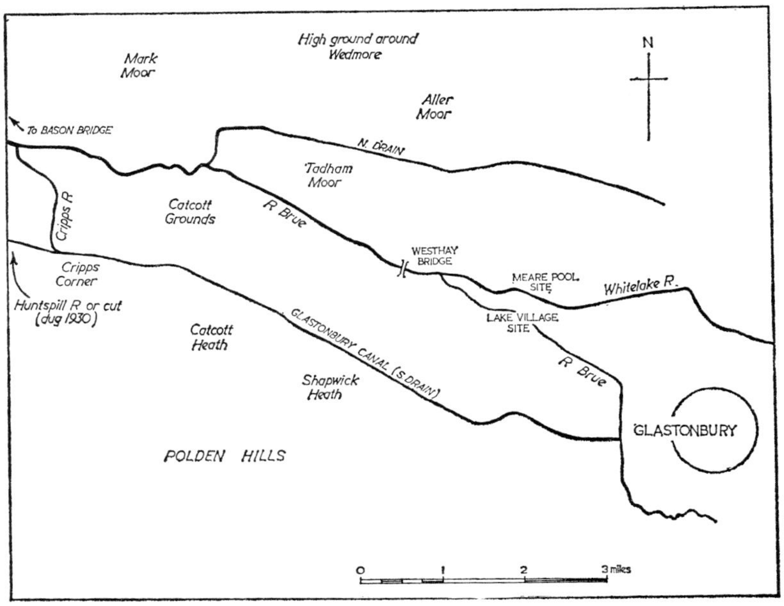

The River Brue drainage schemes.

King's Sedgemoor

Schemes to drain King's Sedgemoor were meanwhile being suggested. In 1775 the idea of draining the whole area was revived by a Mr Allen, MP for Bridgwater. Although this was opposed at a public meeting, it did get some support and there were signs that opinion was moving towards accepting such a scheme. In 1788, local landowner Sir Philip Hales presided at a meeting in Wells, where the idea was again received with abuse and opposi-

Work being carried out on King's Sedgemoor Drain as part of a modern widening scheme.

tion from 'the lower order of commoners'; but he persevered and was able to make an application to Parliament in 1790. By the spring of 1791 a Bill was passed into law, and the commissioners appointed to see that the drainage scheme was carried out held a meeting at Bridgwater. Billingsley, describing in 1795 the background to these events, makes the following comment: 'I have been thus particular in stating the progress of this business merely to show the impropriety of calling a publick meeting with a view of gaining signatures of consent . . . At all publick meetings of this nature that I ever attended noise and clamour have silenced sound sense and argument. Once men have joined the opposition, their pride will not let them relent.'

At this period, the moor drained into the River Parrett some miles above Bridgwater and the first intention was to open and widen the outlets. The fall of water level proved so slight that the commissioners sought a more satisfactory solution. An old sluice, Dunbald Clize, was chosen as a desired drainage point since an 'extraordinary fall of 10ft could be acquired'. Eventually the descent from the upper moor to the sluice gave a fall of 19ft over 12 miles, ie about 1½ft per mile.

This plan was carried out and in 1794 work started on King's Sedgemoor Drain. The old River Cary entered the moor to the north-west of Somerton and then meandered across the Levels. From its point of entry on to the moor at Henley Corner a completely new channel was dug across to the outfall into the River Parrett at Dunball.

Cutting the new drain presented the problem of disposal of the excavated spoil. If it was piled on the banks—which had to be built up—its weight squeezed the soil underneath back into the space that was being cleared out.

To prevent this, the banks had to be very gently sloped. The new cut was 15ft deep, 55ft wide at the top and 10ft wide at the bottom. Even so, there were some bad slides in the early stages until the land settled and became firmer.

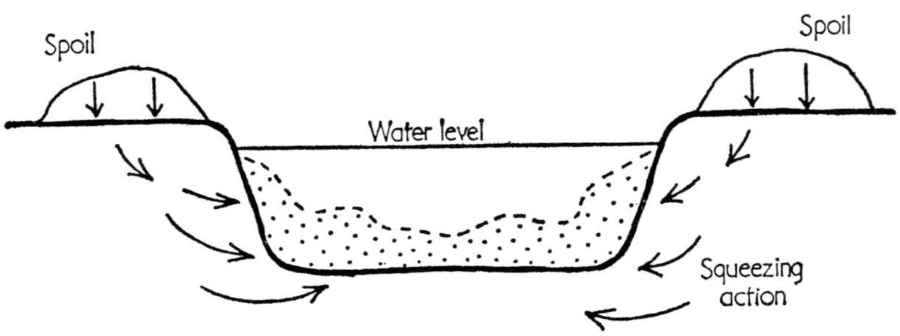

The weight of excavated spoil causes it to squeeze back into the newly cut drain

While the construction work was being carried out, the commissioners were awarded three guineas per day for attendance.

The confluence of the Rivers Parrett and Tone at Burrowbridge. The buildings are on top of the raised banks.

This was ridiculed as being far too much! It was suggested that the work would never be finished since the commissioners would be loath to surrender such an easily earned income. However, the fees were allowed and the final estimates prepared:

Cost of cutting the drain	£ 15,418.	2.	8
Cost of Act of Parliament, clerical fees, interest on borrowed money etc	16,206.	2.	0
Total	£ 31,624.	4.	8
Cost of cutting parish drains	28,000.	0.	0
Original value of the moor	150,000.	0.	0
Grand total	£209,624.	4.	8
After the drainage the value of the moor	575,000.	0.	0
This left an estimated profit of	365,375.	15.	4

Two points about these figures are relevant: first, the estimated value of the land was raised nearly fourfold; second, the fact that the cost of cutting the parochial drains was greater than the outlay on the main drain emphasises the importance of the network as a whole. These subsidiary drains included five which were 18ft wide at the top. These served Shapwick, Street, Aller, Chedzoy (and took their names) and the area to the north-east of Greylake Bridge, where the drain was simply called 'the eighteen foot rhyne'. Smaller drains were cut 12ft wide at the top, 4ft wide at the bottom and 6ft deep.

The cost of cutting was estimated on the assumption that a good workman would earn 3s (15p) per day in summer and 2s (10p) per day in winter. A typical farm labourer, depending on the season, was paid between 1s (5p) and 1s 4d (7p) per day, plus cider; and a woman was paid between 6d (2½p) and 8d (3p) per day, again plus cider. Mowing was paid at the rate of 1s 4d (7p) per acre plus one gallon of cider. In the circumstances, the pay offered to the ditch diggers was comparatively high.

With improved drainage, wheat and oats were sown on the reclaimed land. The value of the land rose from 10s (50p) to 35s (£1.75) an acre. However, repeated ploughing and burning, and the effect of drainage itself, lowered the land level and the ground became too soft. By 1830 a good deal of it was exhausted by overcropping. It was then sown with clover, but since it was too wet for cattle to graze on it, the clover was cropped. Thus no manure was returned to the soil to improve it. Some root crops were planted, by spade because the land was too wet to be cultivated by horse and plough. In bad years farming on the moor was impossible and much of it reverted to rough summer grazing.

The Axe Valley

In the Axe Valley, flooding was less frequent and less damaging. In 1802 a drainage act was passed relating to the Rivers Axe and Yeo, and by 1810 some of the large meanders at Bleadon and Crab Hole were eliminated. A controlling clyce was built and by 1826 it was recorded that 'the flat which was formerly covered with water now affords some of the richest land in the kingdom'. By then the land had settled into the dairy farming pattern that is present today.

South Moor

The South Moor, drained by the Rivers Parrett, Tone, Yeo and Ivel was the last to be reclaimed. Gravitational drainage was impossible here as the River Parrett was narrow, winding and shallow—all the worst attributes for a drainage river, and the water had to be pumped.

The first part of the South Moor to be drained was the Weston Levels, where steam pumping began in 1830. In 1837, a second pumping station was opened at Saltmoor. The agricultural pattern in these areas closely followed that of King's Sedgemoor.

The agricultural depression of the twenty years following 1815 had its effect on the Levels. Schemes which might have been pushed ahead lapsed and the situation was worsened by administrative limitations. As new works built under the enclosure acts and comprehensive drainage acts were completed, they were handed over to the Court of Sewers, the administering body. This court appointed juries of local landowners to supervise maintenance of the drains and report offences against the acts. Unfortunately its threats were innocuous and its administration tardy. As the various acts omitted to include the upper river catchment areas, even an efficient and willing Court of Sewers was restricted in the work it could do.

Drainage work in the twentieth century

Drainage schemes on the Levels progressed very slowly and received little impetus until the present century when the pumping stations were modernised; in the 1940s they began to switch to diesel engines and were extended so that by the 1960s the River Parrett drained over 360,000 acres.

In 1930 the Somerset Rivers Catchment Board was constituted to cover the whole region. When the Royal Ordnance Factory at Puriton, in the River Brue area, grew in size, needing some 4½ million gallons of water per day, the Board inaugurated a combined water supply and drainage scheme. A new drain, the Huntspill Cut, which linked with the old South Drain, could not be dug to the required depth because of the soft soil; therefore gravitational drainage was not sufficient to provide the necessary amount of water. A pumping station was built at Gold Corner, which not only gave the ordnance factory the water it needed, but eliminated winter flooding on this section of the moor.

In 1939–43, improvements were made to King's Sedgemoor Drain, which was widened to about 36ft at the bottom and 80ft at moor level. The catchment area was increased to nearly fifty thousand acres and King's Sedgemoor, the area which it drains directly, is about nine thousand acres (fourteen square miles). Since then there have been sporadic attempts to grow arable crops and most of the area is now pasture, carrying dairy cattle. With general improvement, the sale value of the land drained by King's Sedgemoor Drain is nowadays close to £1 million.*

* 1970 figures.

From the mid-1960s the drainage of the Rivers Tone and Parrett has been much improved; the River Tone has been straightened and its banks strengthened, while new pumping stations built on the upper reaches of the River Parrett have helped to drain the moors around Muchelney. A channel is being cut from the Parrett through to King's Sedgemoor Drain. Thus the flood water from the moors around Langport will be pumped into the River Parrett, channelled across the moors to King's Sedgemoor Drain and thence out to the Parrett estuary at Dunball. To cope with the increased volume of water, King's Sedgemoor Drain is again being widened over much of its length. This scheme should complete the drainage of the moors.

The navigable waterways

While the channels and cuts were being dug to drain and improve the land, a number of plans for canals and waterways were proposed. The main period of canal-building schemes was from the end of the eighteenth century to the middle of the nineteenth, though much of this was limited to committee meetings and surveys; relatively little actual building took place.

The absence of any appreciable high land between the Somerset coast on the Bristol Channel and the Devon/Dorset coast on the English Channel encouraged the production of several schemes for a canal to link the two coasts. This Two-Channel link-up would have made it possible to ship coal from South Wales to London and the Continent without having to take it round the Cornish peninsula.

As early as 1768 a group of Taunton men asked for a survey; Robert Whitworth planned a route from Uphill through Axbridge, Wells, Glastonbury, Bridgwater and Burrowbridge by canal and then by the River Tone to Taunton, from where the route went south-west to Exeter. This was to be called the Exeter–Uphill canal, but the idea came to nothing.

At about the same time, a second route from the River Parrett, near Langport, south through Chard to Seaton was examined, but, again, nothing came of it.

By 1794 yet another route had been surveyed. This ran from Uphill to the collieries near Nailsea, then through Congresbury, Huntspill, Bridgwater, Creech St Michael, Ilminster, Chard and down to Axmouth.

Meanwhile, there was much debate as to whether or not such a canal system linking the Bristol and English Channels would be more rewarding than another proposition, the Grand Western Canal, which would carry 50-ton barges from Exeter via Taunton

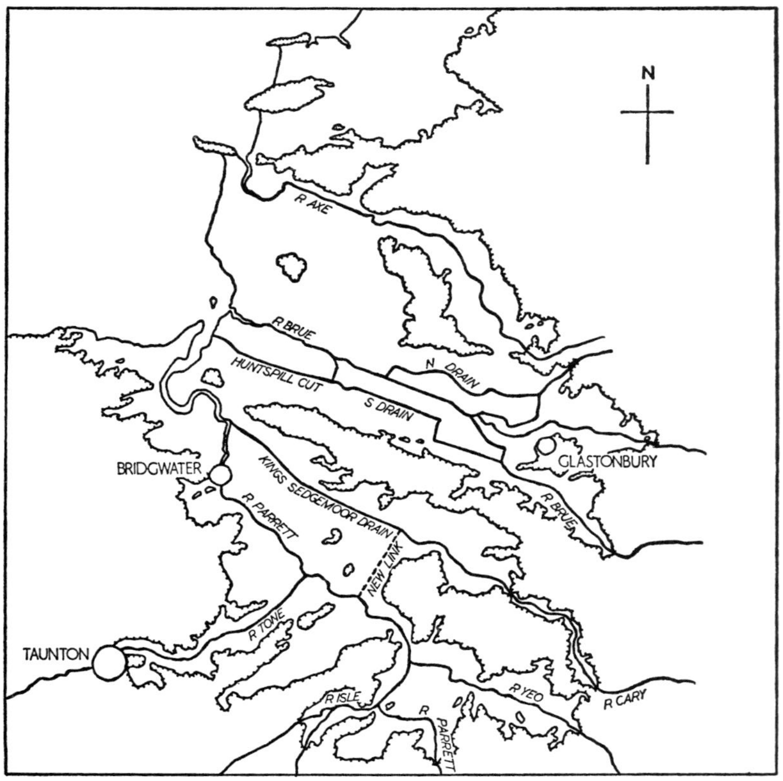

The main navigable waterways, natural and man-made, across the Levels.

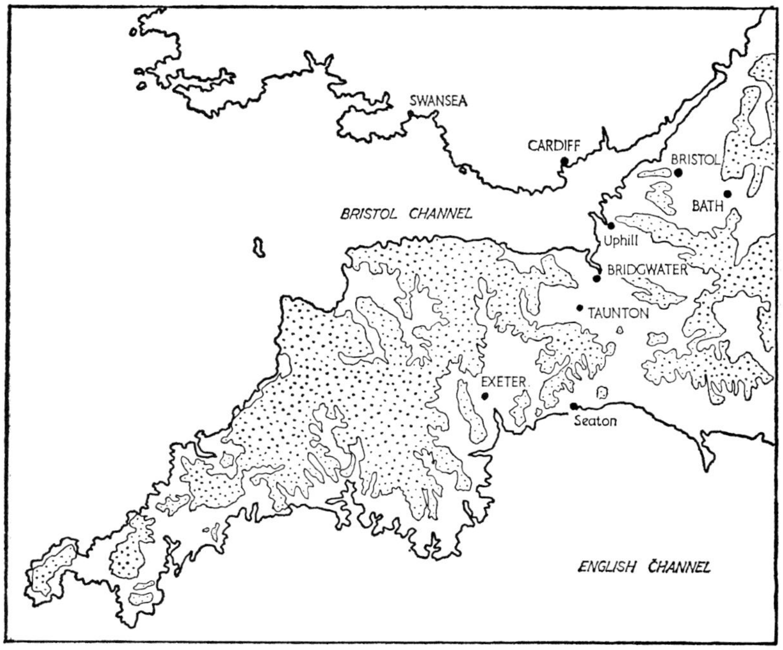

The area through which it was proposed to build canal routes linking the Bristol Channel with the English Channel in the Two-Channels schemes.

and Bristol to London. The outcome resulted in the Two-Channels scheme lying dormant until 1809. When the River Parrett–Chard–Seaton plan had been costed, it was suggested that an outlay of £70,000 would bring a revenue of £30,250 per year! A new survey to build a Two-Channels canal suitable for small coastal vessels came up with rather a different set of figures. This small-ship canal was to start from a wet dock at Combwich, follow the River Parrett to Langport, then cut down to Chard and Seaton to a dock and harbour at Beer. The estimated cost was £1,330,084.

This plan also lapsed, but was revived in 1821. The original route was to be used, this time for tub boats of about four or five tons. The plan was to concentrate on this local shipping, rather than the large colliers envisaged in the earlier scheme, and by doing so to cut down on the initial cost. With some modifications at the northern end, the scheme was expected to need an outlay of about £125,000.

In the next two years, both canal and railway speculation increased; the tub-boat plan was withdrawn and opinion swung back to the idea of a ship canal. Thomas Telford, asked to do a new survey, suggested a ship canal from Stolford to Beer; including the two harbours, the cost was calculated at £1,712,844, with an annual expenditure of £22,000 and an income of £210,847 per year.

As usual, there was opposition to the scheme, this time from the farmers and landowners. It was also claimed that by cutting out the Land's End circuit 'that great nursery for hardy and intrepid seamen' would be destroyed. On the other hand, an

Simplified plan of the suggested routes across Sedgemoor in the projected Two-Channels schemes.

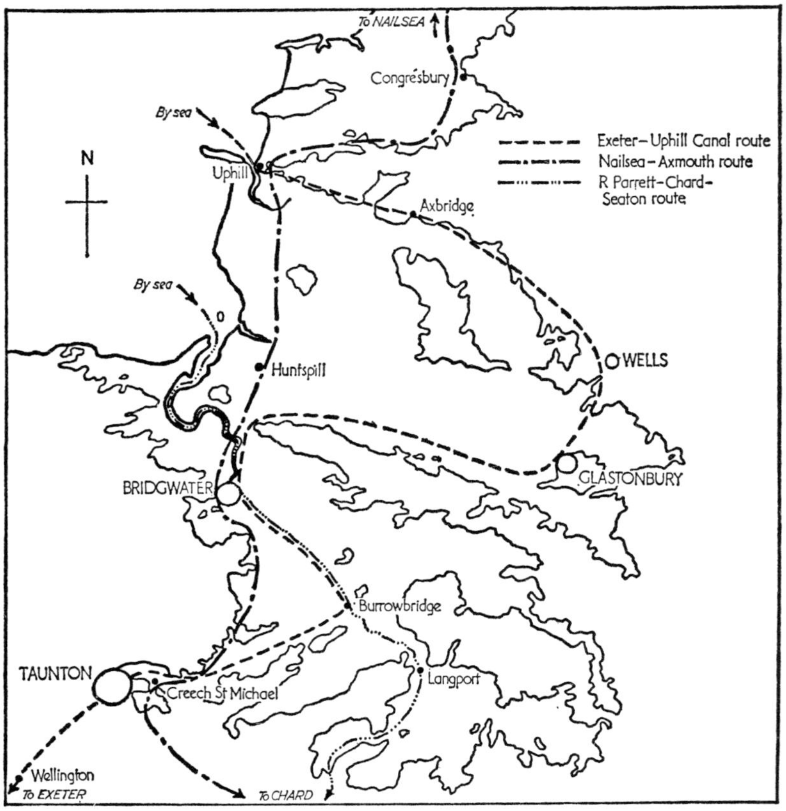

earlier report supporting the Two-Channels scheme suggested that about 200 men were lost each year in making the voyage round Land's End!

Despite opposition, an act for the English and Bristol Channels Ship Canal was passed in 1825, but by this time the boom conditions were fading and the enthusiasm was over. Apart from one more survey in 1828 to reconsider the possibility of a canal for small ships, the Two-Channels scheme died with the act which was intended to give it birth.

As the railway network developed, the idea of joining the two channels again took hold, with a suggested rail link, but the proposed route was to the west of Sedgemoor. Other schemes kept cropping up, but the Bristol–Exeter railway line in its various stages was, and still is, the only connecting route apart from the road.

The Parrett Basin

The River Parrett and the River Tone had long been used as waterways, but when the development of canals and water traffic was in progress there was a revival of interest in these two rivers, both as direct waterways and as part of a wider network.

On the River Parrett, only the smallest boats could get through the bridge at Langport. By 1795 an act was obtained

Bridgwater about 1870. Sea going vessels unloaded their cargo into river/canal barges for transport further inland.

authorising a canal of some eight miles which would run from just below Langport to Ilchester. In the next two years work was put in hand to by-pass the bridge by using the Portlake rhyne and extending it for about three-quarters of a mile. The money ran out before this job was finished and, as in earlier days, goods still had to be manhandled from the larger boats working downstream of Langport to the smaller ones capable of getting up the River Yeo. This use of Langport as a 'staging post' brought a good deal of prosperity to the town and in the first thirty years of the nineteenth century its population rose from about 750 to about 1,250 (by the middle of this century the figure had gone down to about 650). Once the goods were upstream of Langport, they could go up to the warehouse at Load Bridge or on to Pill Bridge just outside Ilchester.

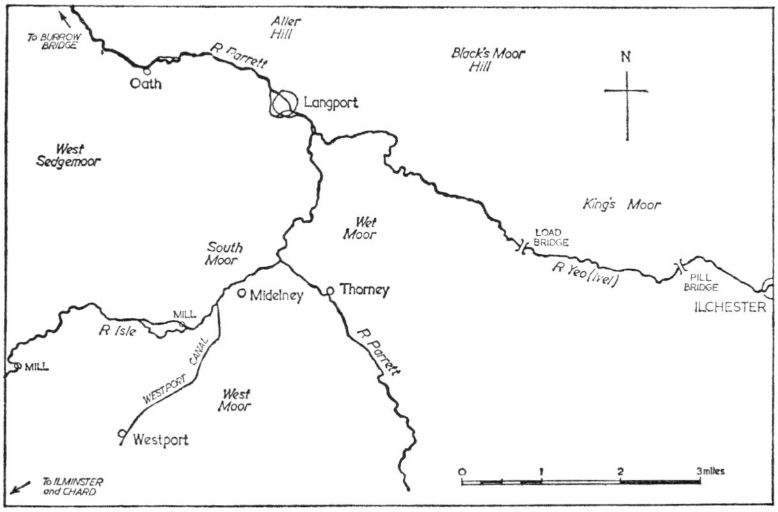

The upper reaches of the River Parrett, showing navigable routes.

A view of Langport from the River Parrett.

The rival waterway routes of the Bridgwater-Taunton Canal and the rivers Parrett and Tone.

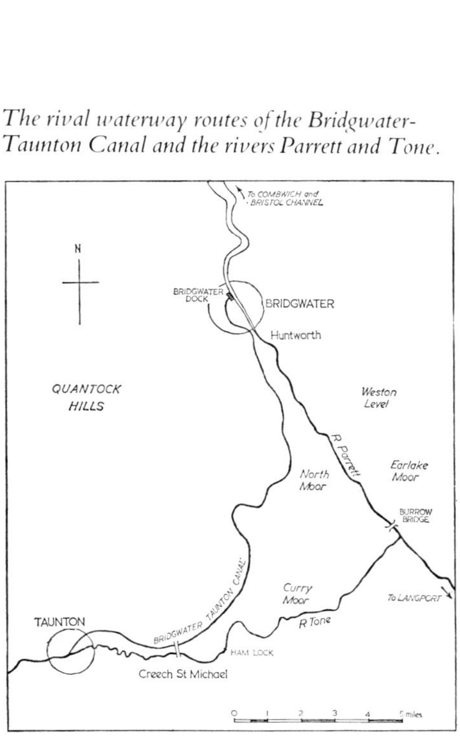

To the south-west of Langport, the River Isle made the idea of a link with Ilminster and Chard a possibility, which finally became reality with the cutting of the Westport Canal. This whole operation, completed in 1840, involved several locks, one of them at Oath, where the River Parrett ceased to be tidal. Langport bridge was rebuilt and the canal cut from the River Isle, near Midelney, through West Moor down to Westport, where wharves were built for goods to be unloaded before being taken on by road to Ilminster and beyond.

At the beginning, this proved quite a profitable concern; tolls amounted to more than £2,000 in the first year and about 70,000 tons of goods were carried annually. Its success led to a revival of interest in making the River Yeo navigable to Ilchester, but this idea was not pursued.

As elsewhere, the developing railway system successfully competed with the canals, and when the Yeovil, Langport and Taunton rail link was opened in 1853 there was a rapid drop in canal traffic; by 1857 the canal tolls were less than £700.

Maintenance of some canals clashed with efforts to improve the drainage. As long as the canal was prosperous and carrying plenty of traffic, there seems to have been no problem, but when it ceased to be busy financial difficulties arose. In addition, the lock at Oath was not allowing sufficient water to escape and when, in the 1870s, West Moor flooded, the lock gates were held open and the canal functioned more as a drain. When the Westport Canal fell into disuse, shipping on the River Parrett upstream of Bridgwater became less and less frequent; the last reference to barges coming up to Oath is in 1911.

The River Tone complex and the Chard Canal

Further upstream from the Langport complex, the River Tone enters the River Parrett at Burrowbridge. This waterway seems to have been first utilised in the mid-seventeenth century, when barges went up on the tide as far as Ham Mills, about three miles from Taunton. By the end of that century, a group called the Tone Conservators had been formed with the object of making the River Tone navigable right into the town. The aim was to make this a financial success and devote the profit to the poor of Taunton.

By 1717 the river was navigable for barges of up to fifteen tons, though the last three miles to Taunton still presented difficulties. The main cargo was coal from South Wales and Bristol, and there are records of iron, wine, flax and pitch also being carried. Though there was a steady growth in trade, payments to the original developers and the cost of making and keeping the river navigable precluded any donations being made to the poor of Tauntons However, the Conservators did impose one restraint on themselve. when they decided, on their annual 'view of the River', to limit the cost of their dinner to 6s (30p) per head.

By the beginning of the nineteenth century, some 14,000 tons of goods were being carried, about 11,500 tons of which was coal transported to Taunton. Four full locks and four half locks were built, and there were various schemes to enlarge the system, especially by linking with the projected Grand Western Canal and ultimately having connections with Exeter and London as well as an outlet into the Bristol Channel. Once again there were objections from farmers and landowners who were afraid the schemes would affect either the drainage or water supply to their land.

However, two schemes did materialise, at least in part. In 1810, a canal was started to link Taunton with the River Exe, and in 1827 the Bridgwater–Taunton Canal was opened. Originally planned as part of a Bristol–Taunton waterway, this canal would have gone right across Sedgemoor from Banwell (where it was to emerge from a tunnel) down to Bridgwater. From there, it was to go on to Taunton, skirting the Quantock edge of Sedgemoor. The scheme was very ambitious and involved crossing the Rivers Axe, Brue and Parrett by aqueducts.

Those concerned with Sedgemoor drainage were apprehensive and, when the appropriate act was passed in 1811, a clause was inserted preventing the canal company from cutting any part between Clevedon and the River Parrett until the sections at each end had been completed. A time limit was also written into the act and the work had to be completed in four years.

Nothing was done and, when the four years were up, plans to go across Sedgemoor were dropped. However, part of this scheme, south of Bridgwater, did proceed and 200 navigators were employed to cut the canal from Huntworth to Taunton. After several setbacks, the work was completed by 1827. Naturally, the canal was competitive with the River Tone and a price war followed. With about 90,000 tons of traffic per year being carried up the waterways, at least as far as Ham Mills, the two authorities considered that this was trade worth fighting for. Tolls on the river, which had been 4s (20p) for three tons were reduced to 1s 6d (7½p). The canal authorities replied by taking over control of the river; they occupied the river superintendent's cottage, increased canal and river tolls, and allowed the maintenance of the river to fall below standard. After taking legal action, the Tone Conservators regained control; they cut the river tolls and further retaliated by keeping the canal short of water. The wrangles were finally settled in 1832 in favour of the canal authorities, on condition that they put the river in good navigable order and maintained it. This was duly done and the river normally carried about 13,000 tons of traffic.

When the Chard Canal was opened in 1842, much of this river traffic went on to Ilminster. In turn this led to an increase in the use of the Bridgwater–Taunton Canal, as larger craft could be used for the through journey. With this switch to the canal, the river traffic declined to less than 2,000 tons in 1870.

Meanwhile, the port of Bridgwater was expanding and by the 1830s it was handling over 120,000 tons. By 1841 a canal loop had been built through the town itself; the company had closed the Huntworth basin and opened Bridgwater Dock. By 1844 the Bristol–Exeter railway was open and connected by horse tramway with the docks at Bridgwater and Dunball. More traffic switched to the railways and, in 1866, the railway company bought the Bridgwater–Taunton Canal for £64,000. In the 1870s the docks at Bridgwater and Dunball had a direct rail connection with the main line and by this time were handling nearly a quarter of a million tons of goods annually. However, this prosperity was relatively shortlived. When the Severn Tunnel was opened in 1886, there was a rapid drop in sea traffic, affecting the Bristol Channel ports. By 1905 the Bridgwater–Taunton Canal tonnage had dropped to 6,420 tons and by 1907 it ceased. River traffic fell too; the last barge to go up to Burrowbridge was in 1928. During World War II the swing-bridges on the canal were replaced by fixed bridges. Sea traffic continued into Bridgwater Dock, mostly bringing timber from Scandinavia, but gradually declined and the docks were closed in 1968.

Over the last few years it has been proposed that the canal should be used as a 'leisure way', for canoeing, angling and other pastimes. Schemes have also been put forward to make use of the dock site.

When the Bridgwater—Taunton Canal was opened in 1827, Chard businessmen considered the possibility of a waterway link with their town, and in 1842 the Chard Canal came into being. It went from Creech St Michael, near Taunton, across West Moor to a lift at Thornfalcon, where it went down and across the south-western tip of West Sedgemoor to another lift at Wrantage, completing its route through to Ilminster and Chard.

The canal was designed for boats 26ft long by 6ft wide, which carried coal up to Ilminster and Chard, and wool on the return journey. However, with the opening of the Taunton–Chard railway line in 1866, the canal could no longer be run profitably and was closed a few years later.

Other canal schemes

Rivalling the Two-Channels scheme in the immensity of its concept was the proposition of a Grand Western Canal, which was planned to take barges of up to 50 tons from Exeter via Taunton and Bristol on to London. The two schemes are very similar in their history in that plans and surveys were made but not much was accomplished. In 1811 some work on the Grand Western was carried out between Taunton and Exeter, but it was not until 1838 that a canal was opened from Taunton to Tiverton and beyond. Like many other ventures, it became involved in a railway price-war and, after a long period of decline, was abandoned in 1962.

Apart from these ambitious schemes, which would have been routed across parts of Sedgemoor, three smaller canals were dug which related much more closely to the Levels: Galton's Canal and Brown's Canal were used to carry silt, and the Glastonbury Canal was an attempt to utilise the existing drainage channel.

In the early nineteenth century Galton dug his canal from the River Brue north-west of Meare up to the North Drain. From the river, a small embanked section was built, then a small lock and finally the canal ran to the Drain at the level of the local rhynes. Brown built a similar canal about one and a half miles downstream. Both were used throughout most of the nineteenth century, but at the end of that period they became incorporated into the drainage board's system and functioned simply as drainage rhynes.

The Glastonbury Canal was built in the 1820s to the south of the River Brue and more or less used the original South Moor Drain, running from Glastonbury, along South Moor Drain to Cripp's Corner. Here it turned northwards and met the River Brue about a mile upstream of Bason Bridge. The lock gates, just above Highbridge, were used as sea locks and could be opened during flooding to release the inland flood water.

The Glastonbury Canal was opened in 1833, but within twenty years it was taken over by the railway. During its independent existence, it was not well maintained and the bottom became silted up. As a simple solution the lock gates at Highbridge were closed, so that they penned back more water. This increased the depth in the canal, but destroyed its drainage value, with the inevitable result that the land flooded. In 1850 the lock gates were reopened and the waterway reverted to its original function as a drain.

In 1852 the railway to Glastonbury and beyond was built along the canal bank and, almost adding insult to injury, the canal was used to bring in the chippings needed for its construction. It is interesting to note that faggots were used to make the railway track firm; the track-laying techniques had altered little in 5,000 years.

The motorist who occasionally goes off the road today and finishes up in the ditch may find some consolation from this story about the Glastonbury line related by R. Atthill: one foggy morning, a light petrol engine was hauling a couple of peat trucks when it stalled on the Peat Companies' crossing. After attempting to uncouple his trucks, the driver ran down the line to warn an approaching train. Owing to the fog, he was not seen and a crash occurred. The train's engine was derailed and shot into the mud of the drain at the side of the line. It was then found impossible to position the heavy crane that was needed to lift the engine without a lot of pile-driving to form a firm base over the peat bog. Instead, the drain was temporarily diverted whilst the engine was cut up into relatively small pieces for removal to the scrap heap!

However, the opening of the railway meant the closing of the canal and eventually, in 1966, the railway itself was closed.

Following a derailment near Ashcott, the engine fell from the line and became stuck in the adjacent ditch.

Haymaking when horses and men provided the labour.

At about the time the canal was being built, a local farmer named Morris attempted to use the silt deposited on the banks of the River Brue. He opened a gap, controlled by sluices, level with the bottom of the river. From the gap he cut a drain about three-quarters of a mile long and when a flood was imminent he opened the sluice. This allowed the River Brue to escape and carry silt with it. As the silt settled out, the 'thinned' flood emptied back into the river through a return rhyne. This method of fertilising the land may have had a little local success, but it does not seem to have been copied and in fact soon died out.

The modified natural pattern

With the establishment of this maze of man-made drainage and navigation waterways, the old succession–flooding cycle was disrupted and a new pattern emerged. Over much of the Levels, improved drainage meant that plant succession moved forward a little way and land became firmer. However, once it became dry enough to support a grassland community, cattle were introduced and normal sequence was artificially held back, since any tree or shrub seedlings which may have germinated were grazed out by the cattle and the moors became a land of permanent pasture. This could have led to the disappearance of those established plants which needed open water or very marshy conditions; but the very drainage pattern which provides the pastures demands a network of ditches. In this way the formerly wild, wet land has been replaced by a man-controlled ditch area. The plants which need open water can grow in the centre of the ditch, those which require marshy conditions can survive at its banks. The flooding which prevented too big a build-up of dead organic material has been replaced by the ditch-clearer and the tractor-operated dredger. At any one moment on the Levels can be found the

The old natural cycle of succession and flooding. The time taken to complete the cycle would have depended on the climate and precise location of the site. The shortest path, taking about one year, was probably the most common; the longer paths took several years.

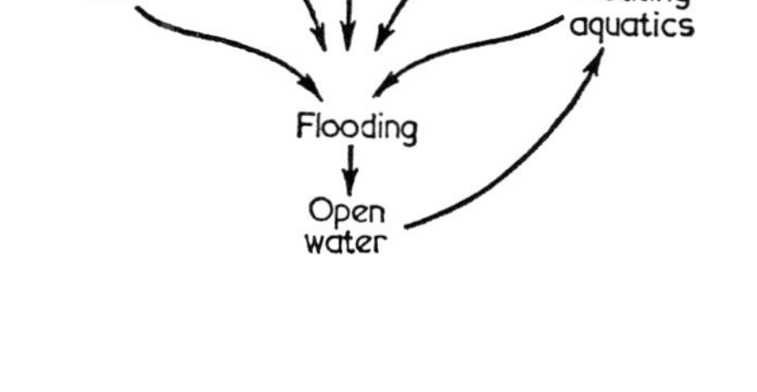

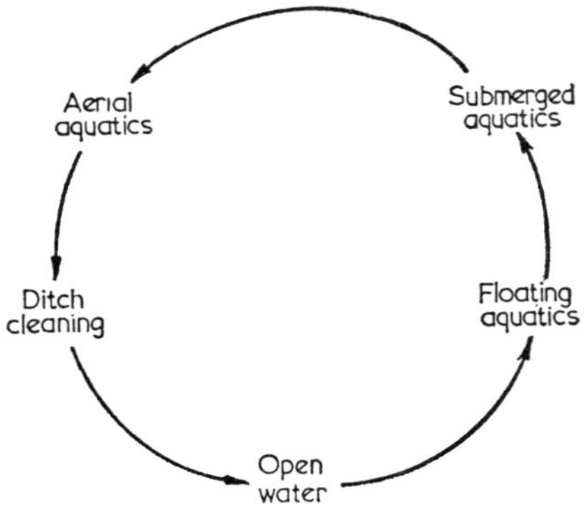

The modern cycle of drain and ditch clearing. This takes some four to six years to complete.

ditch which has just been cleared, the one which is well established and the one which is shortly due for reclearing. In this way the ditches, man-made and man-controlled, are the descendants of the natural patches of open water which have always been present.

This means that many of the old plants have survived and the area remains for the moment remarkably rich in aquatic and marshy plants. Though none is unique to the Somerset Levels, many otherwise uncommon plants grow here in abundance. People are becoming familiar with names like *Hottonia palustris*, the Water Violet, which is advertised as suitable for planting at the edges of garden pools. Here one can find a hundred-yard stretch of ditch absolutely smothered in it.

Just as plants survive in this man-made habitat, so do most of the animals. The open water provides a habitat for many invertebrates as well as fish, frogs and newts. As the succession developed, so these were succeeded by marsh living forms. As the old marsh gave way to carr, so there was a corresponding change in animal life. The insect with an aquatic larva was replaced by one whose caterpillar was adapted to eating alder and willow leaves; and the snipe was replaced by the insectivorous warbler. In the past, all these animals lived more or less side by side, some part of the moor always being wet enough to provide the optimum habitat. The coming of the drainage schemes affected the animal life to some extent. The narrow strip at the side of a ditch is often too restricted for some animals, which need not only a feeding ground but also nesting sites and cover from predators.

The old pattern of succession-flooding with its unique flora and fauna has been replaced by the modern pattern, with pasture, and occasionally arable, land, drained by a system of ditches and artificial waterways. Most of the relatively uncommon plants have so far survived and many of the associated animals are 'hanging on'. However, over the past ten years, this pattern has been undergoing further change. Ditch-clearing is rarely done by hand; tractors and dredgers carry out the work more quickly, clearing a bigger area at a time. A plant growing in a particular place can be completely removed within a few days; in the past, when ditch-clearing took longer, a plant could 'leapfrog' to a safer spot. Not only mechanisation, but the use of herbicides and pesticides constitutes a hazard to wild life, though fortunately such spraying is uncommon on the Levels. Larger areas of land are now under control, in some places the ditches being filled in to form more extensive fields. As the drainage improves, so more land is being ploughed and cropped. The overall effect on this unique landscape of Sedgemoor will be its loss of distinctive character and a merging into the dull uniformity which is transforming so much of the countryside.

Grazing on the Levels today. The hill in the background is Burrow Mump.

4
Plant Life of the Sedgemoor Fen

The scientific names of plants are those used by Clapham, Tutin & Warburg in *Flora of the British Isles* (Cambridge, 1958). I appreciate that there have been some changes in nomenclature since then but feel that, for general use, it is more convenient to keep to one authority throughout. A new *Flora of Somerset* was published in 1981. This should be consulted for the latest information on the status of plants in the County.

With its habitats ranging from open water to scrub woodland, and from alkaline fen to acid bog, Sedgemoor has a rich and varied plant life; some plants which are rare in other parts of England are common in this area.

In looking first at the plants of the fens, a clearer picture can be obtained by following the sequence of plant life in the ditches, rather than adopting the traditional means of considering each botanical family in turn.

The first plants to colonise the open water are usually the floating aquatic plants, which are frequently carried in by water currents or regenerate from odd scraps left behind when the ditch is cleaned. This may take the form of new shoots developing, or by growth and division. Many plants have the ability to reproduce vegetatively, ie without producing seeds. New 'shoots' develop from the original plant and produce their own roots. Gradually their dependence on the parent breaks down, the connecting tissues wither away and the 'shoots' become independent young plants. Occasionally new plants are introduced by animals; cattle, drinking from a ditch, put their fore-feet into the water and plants, or parts of them, adhere around the hooves. When the cattle drink from another ditch, the plant material is loosened into the water.

By far the commonest family in this group is the Duckweed family (*Lemna* spp); frequently occurring with the Duckweeds is Frog-bit (*Hydrocharis morsus-ranae*). Sometimes found in large quantities but in rather restricted areas is the Water Fern (*Azolla filiculoides*), which was introduced into England in 1910 and quickly

*Californian Water Fern (*Azolla filiculioides*) spread in to the ditches at the beginning of this century. It now occurs in patches over much of the area.*

spread to Sedgemoor. The green algae, generally lumped together under the name Blanket Weed, are also common.

In the life cycle of these floating aquatic plants there are three main dangers: the destruction of their open water habitat by the natural process of succession; the carrying away of plants by water currents; and the risk of surface-floating plants being frozen into the winter ice.

Losses due to the first two hazards are made up by a very rapid vegetative growth. To avoid the last danger, these plants have developed a pattern whereby they build up starch at the surface of the water during the summer months, these chemical changes making the small plants dense enough to sink down in the autumn. Although many of them die, a sufficient number survive and lie dormant on the bottom. Sometimes, as with the Duckweeds, it is the entire plant which sinks and remains dormant; in Frog-bit it is the turions or special winter buds (see page 54), and in the algae this period is passed in a resting spore stage. As the temperature rises in the following spring, the starch is broken down. This liberates energy, which the plants use in growth, and at the same time the density is reduced so that the plants float up to the surface. Not only does this method give protection during the winter, but it also helps in the struggle for space; the blankets of Duckweed descending on to the submerged plants have a deleterious effect on them.

The submerged aquatic plants such as the Pondweeds (*Potamogeton* spp) and Starworts (*Callitriche* spp) usually grow up from fragments remaining after the ditches are cleaned. In general, the plants are much branched and fairly brittle; this brittleness, partly due to the air spaces in the stems, would be a handicap in fast-flowing water. However, in the Sedgemoor ditches, the flow of water is so slight that it does little harm. On the other hand, when the ditches are cleaned, the plants break up and sufficient remnants are left behind to enable a new population to grow up.

Rather slower to become established are those aquatic plants which carry most of their leaves and flowers above the water. Typical of this group are the sedges (*Carex* spp) and the Water Plantain (*Alisma plantago-aquatica*). On the other hand, such species as the Water Violet (*Hottonia palustris*) with only their tall flowering stems held above the water surface emphasise that in nature there is no sharp dividing line.

The species in this group are not very numerous. However, until the drainage schemes took effect, it was this group that dominated the whole area. These plants not only tolerate flooding, but are specially adapted to thrive in such conditions. For the majority of them, the ideal habitat is one where, for at least part of the year, the ground is covered with water. At the same time, the plants could thrive during the dry summers when the water was almost dried up.

Fortunately many of these species can still survive in the existing rhynes and ill-drained areas. Sedges and rushes are usually to be found at the edges of the rhynes, while Bur-reeds (*Sparganium* spp) and Water Plantains do best in open water made shallower by preceding types of vegetation. The majority of the plants in this group are monocotyledons. Usually several feet high, they are sometimes called the 'upright swamp association'. These narrow-leaved, tall plants are especially well adapted to these conditions; their stems and leaves contain large air spaces carrying oxygen from the air down to their underwater organs. The young plants can push their lance-shaped leaves through surrounding vegetation and their eventual height benefits them in the competition for sunlight. Even a few broad-leaved plants, such as Great Water Dock (*Rumex hydrolapathum*), have their young leaves rolled in on themselves, so that they appear cylindrical; once they have penetrated the lower vegetation the leaves unroll and take up a more normal dock-leaf shape.

With some few exceptions among the dicotyledons, these plants with their roots in the water and their leaves in the air are not a showy group. The majority of the flowers are wind-pollinated and petal-less, but they have a quiet beauty of their own: the glorious reddish purple of the opening reed heads, the stateliness of the Reedmace, the delicacy of the flowers of the Reed-grasses and the gold, black and silver 'candelabra' of the Bur-reeds.

Normally the development of this group marks the turning point in the ditch cycle; it is at this stage that the ditch is cleaned out, but, if the cleaning is delayed and no cattle are introduced, then the alder and willow carr can succeed. The freshness of the opening alder leaves and the powder-puffs of the 'pussy willow' have their own charm. Unfortunately, as ditch-clearing became mechanised, many of these trees have been grubbed out. Plenty still survive, but the general tendency is for the ditches to become less tree-lined every year.

*A ditch showing both the flat floating leaves of Frog-bit (*Hydrocharis mosus-ranae*) and the short spires of Water Violet (*Hottonia palustris*).*

A ditch showing a typical mixture of aquatic and marsh loving plants.

In order to get some idea of the frequency with which the different plant species occur, the ditches have been divided into four age groups:

(1) Newly cleaned, ie within the last month or two in summer or within a maximum of six months, if they are cleaned out in the late autumn. The banks are cleared of vegetation.

(2) Recently cleaned; with about seventy-five per cent of the original surface 'open' (ie usually either open water or with only floating aquatic plants growing on it).

(3) Middle-aged; with about fifty per cent or a little less of the surface open.

(4) Old; where the ditches are so overgrown that there is less than twenty-five per cent of the surface open.

In a series of recordings, each ditch was judged 'by eye' and put into one of these four groups. An arbitrary position was chosen on the bank and a note made of all the plants which grew across the ditch in line with the mark. The plants were recorded on a 'present or absent' basis and no attempt was made to estimate their numbers or the proportion of the ditch occupied by them. The process was then repeated further along the ditch, with a minimum of ten paces between each recording and no more than ten recordings to any one stretch of ditch. This was to avoid a situation whereby one ditch, running alongside a drove for, say, half a mile, and which had been cleaned in one continuous operation, could 'dominate' the results. Although the work was centred around Westonzoyland, it covered most of the moor south of the Polden Hills. Originally, 100 counts were made on the 'recently cleaned' ditches. These were then repeated on another part of the moor and the two sets of results were compared. They showed some degree of correlation, but not enough to be statistically valid. A third count was made of another 200 ditches and this was compared with the total from the first two counts. This

*The distinctive leaves and flowers of Arrow-head (*Sagittaria sagittifolia*). Frog-bit and Duckweed are floating on the water surface.*

time the correlation was close enough to show that a count of 200 was a large enough sample to give a representative figure. The counts were spread throughout the year, to allow for seasonal variations.

The first table of these results is given below:

PLANTS RECORDED		AGE OF DITCHES			
		Newly cleaned	*Recently cleaned*	*Middle-aged*	*Old*
Lemna minor	Common Duckweed	136	157	143	55
L. gibba	Fat Duckweed	81	81	31	0
L. polyrhiza	Great Duckweed	35	29	9	0
L. triscula	Ivy Duckweed	57	103	84	11
Hydrocharis morsus-ranae	Frog-bit	25	104	69	8
Algae	Blanket-weed	27	38	0	1
Callitriche spp	Starwort	15	21	0	0
Elodea canadensis	Canadian Pondweed	18	21		0
Phalaris arundinacea	Reed-grass	6	98	93	69
Glyceria maxima	Reed-grass	1	28	31	21
Phragmites communis	Reed	3	26	33	36
Sparganium ramosum	Bur-reed	1	43	83*	71
Juncus spp	Rushes	5	66	103	64
Carex spp	Sedges	17	82	79	106
Filipendula ulmaria	Meadow-sweet	6	45	66	51
Urtica dioica	Stinging Nettle	0	57	32	52
Galium palustre	Marsh Bedstraw	1	23	40	50
Iris pseudacorus	Yellow Flag	1	29	25	30
Solanum dulcamara	Bittersweet	0	4	20	10
Rumex hydrolapathum	Great Water Dock	0	13	41	16
Berula erecta	Water-parsnip	11	3	32	19

* Includes 2 counts of *Sparganium simplex*
Plants typical of the adjoining pasture have been excluded

Structure of the Duckweeds.

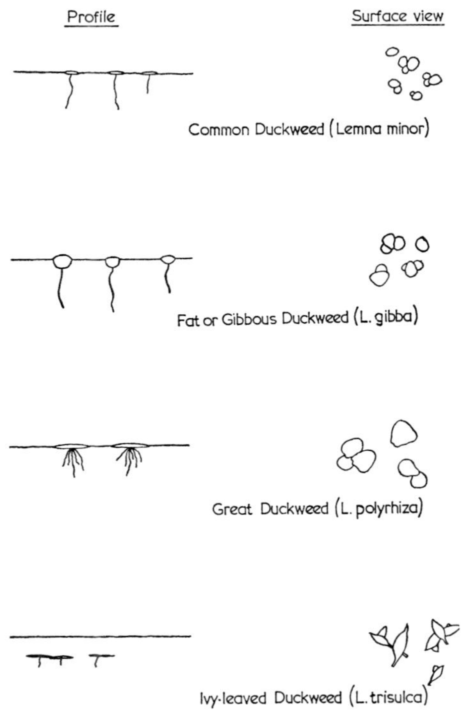

The table shows which plants are numerous at the different stages, and which are less so. Though the table does not give a complete picture, it is reasonable to assume that the more common a plant is, the more likely it is to play an important part in the ecology. I have, therefore, listed first those plants which occur at least twenty times in any one type of ditch. Plants which occur less frequently are listed and described in pages 92–111.

COMMON DUCKWEED (*Lemna minor*) is by far the commonest flowering plant in the ditches. Not only does it occur most frequently throughout much of the ditch cycle, but it occurs in enormous numbers, often covering the entire surface of the open water. In modern ecological work it is usually this coverage which is most important (a hundred small plants may occupy less space than one big one) since it indicates the part the species plays in the energy path. In the early stages of ditch colonisation, it is this plant which traps much of the sun's energy and thereby makes it available to the associated animal population.

FAT OR GIBBOUS DUCKWEED (*L. gibba*) is almost as common in some areas and the two are often found together. Both have only one root, but the undersurface of the thallus of this species is markedly convex. This difference is easy enough to see though its significance is not clear. However, the differences between the two species are such that, while Common Duckweed occurs almost everywhere, Fat Duckweed is much more limited in its distribution.

GREAT DUCKWEED (*L. polyrhiza*) is considerably larger than the other two species, sometimes reaching about one centimetre across. The underside of the thallus is flat and often an unusual purple-green shade. Like the other two species, some of its leaves sink in winter, but it also produces buds which, instead of opening, break off in the autumn and fall to the bottom of the ditch. The following spring, they develop and rise to the surface. One would expect this bigger plant to be more successful, but it is one of the least distributed of the group.

IVY-LEAVED DUCKWEED (*L. triscula*) is quite unlike the rest of the genus. Its leaves are spear-shaped and it floats some few inches below the surface. When this plant becomes established in a ditch, it can completely dominate the vegetation. Like all the duckweeds, it succeeds by cutting off the light from the plants below; even in the height of summer when there is the maximum amount of light, dead and dying plants are sometimes found on the floor of the ditch, killed off because light has been excluded from them. Once this plant has got into a ditch, the lower plants must race against time and grow through the Duckweed before the mosaic of its leaves cuts off their vital sunlight.

FROG-BIT (*Hydrocharis morsus-ranae*) often looks like a small Water-lily. It sometimes shares the dominant position with the Duckweeds and the delicate, three-petalled white flowers look most attractive during the summer. It, too, survives by producing turions, buds which drop off and sink, and in winter a floating Frog-bit leaf is a rarity. Once they reach the surface, the young plants produce runners very similar to those produced by strawberries. This burst of activity usually starts in May, and by July they form an interlocking network across the ditch. Occasionally they reproduce so rapidly that the floating mass is constricted by

Distribution maps of 1. Lemna minor *(Common Duckweed)*; 2. Lemna gibba *(Fat Duckweed)*; 3. Lemna polyrhiza *(Great Duckweed)*; 4. Lemna trisculca *(Ivy-leaved Duckweed)*.

Vertical lines in this and subsequent distribution maps denote 'recorded in the County Flora, 1898, *and supplement,* 1914'. *Horizontal lines denote 'recorded during* 1955-1965'.

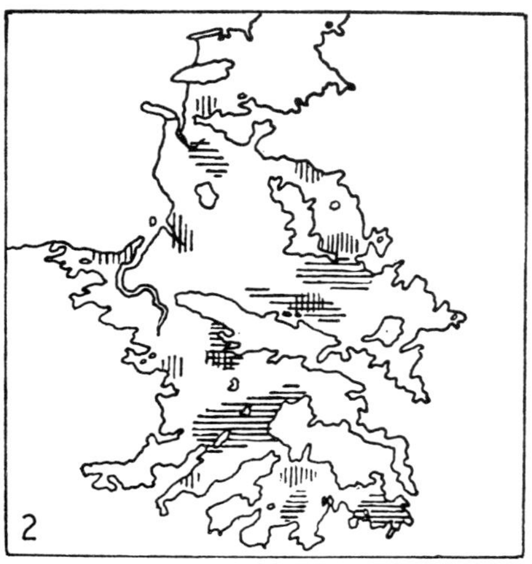

Seasonal development of Frog-bit (Hydrocharis morsus-ranae).

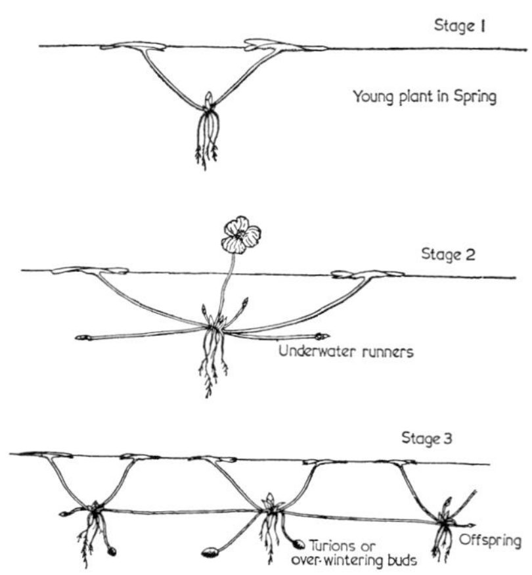

the sides of the ditch and it folds up on itself like a wrinkled blanket.

BLANKET-WEEDS (*Chlorophycaea*) are among the least attractive floating plants. During the summer they look rather like masses of green, floating cotton-wool, and in the autumn, when they have lost their colour and are beginning to decay, they can look quite revolting. The flowerless strands are made of more or less identical cylindrical cells joined end to end, and the group is very closely related to the single-celled microscopic green plants, the unicellular algae (including the desmids). The importance of this group lies in the fact that its members are extremely numerous and trap a good deal of the sunlight falling on the ditches. They use this energy to manufacture their own cell material, such as carbohydrates and proteins, thus providing a grazing ground for many minute forms of animal life. In addition to being one of the first links in this food chain, the Blanket-weeds make an ideal refuge for smaller animals. The larger predatory fish will rarely penetrate into the middle of the 'blanket', so the creatures living there have a comparatively safe home. Altogether, 160 species of algae have been recorded from Sedgemoor.

One of the surprising things about these floating aquatic plants is their scattered distribution. In the County Flora, only the Common Duckweed is described as 'very common', the others occur spasmodically. In the survey I made during 1955–65, I too found their distribution followed no fixed pattern and even varied from year to year. To some extent their distribution must depend on their winter survival, but I suspect that the key factor is the direction of water flow in the ditches. Allied to this is the question of how the ditches are bridged. In some cases the bridges are carried above the surface; Duckweeds can pass under them in the current. In other cases the bridge is an earth bank pierced by drainpipes below the water surface. This often has the effect of trapping the floating plants upstream (and upwind) of these bridges. When the water is allowed into the smaller ditches, especially during summer drought, the distribution of the plants may well depend on which sluice is used and which bridges are upstream of it.

STARWORT (*Callitriche* spp) is a genus described as 'troublesome': it is extremely difficult to separate the different species and the only one identified with certainty is Common Starwort (*C. stagnalis*). The long thin submerged leaves are arranged in opposite pairs, but the terminal leaves float on the surface forming a small rosette. These pale green rosettes which give the plant its name look most attractive, and since the lower leaves are also pale green they show up well in the water. For this reason the plant seems to demonstrate that the aquatic world is a three-dimensional one. A few sticklebacks, swimming amongst the plants and able to move up and down, serve to emphasise this fact.

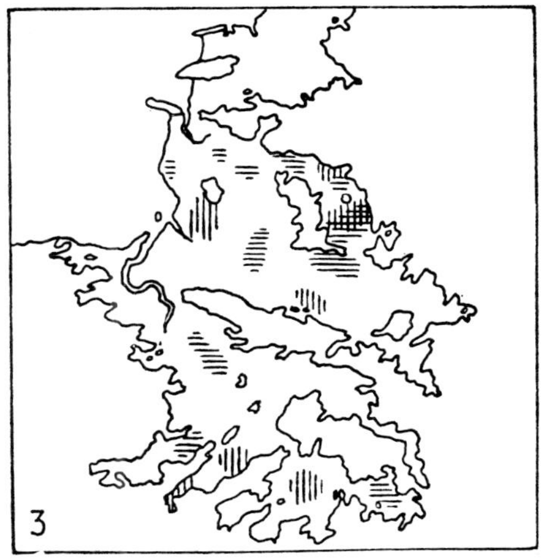

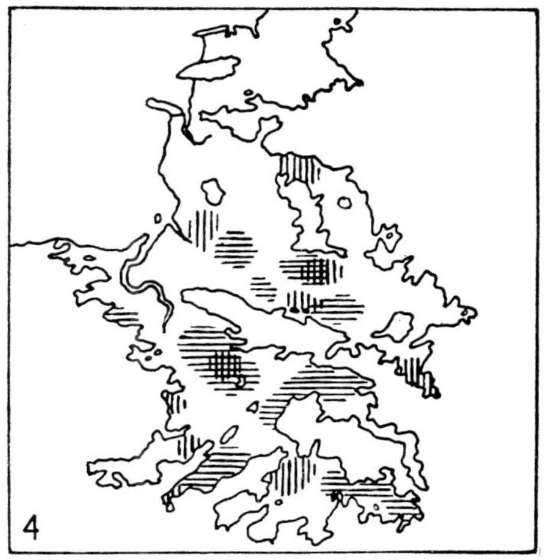

RECORDED IN THE COUNTY FLORA, 1898, AND SUPPLEMENT, 1914

RECORDED DURING 1955-65

CANADIAN PONDWEED (*Elodea canadensis*) is an introduced plant which is now very common amongst the submerged aquatic flora. It was first noted in England in 1847 near Market Harborough, which at that time was something of a centre for the canal systems of the country and the plant spread outwards along these waterways. It grew abundantly and it has been suggested that the extra effort and money involved in keeping the canals clear of it was, in a very mixed metaphor, the straw that tipped the balance from them to the railways. After this first 'flush of enthusiasm', the plant settled into what is more or less its present status. It is likely that in the early stages the plant had a plentiful supply of the nutrient salts which it needed and at the same time relatively few 'enemies'. As the population built up, so the salts became scarcer as they were absorbed and held within the plants, and animal predators adapted to feeding on the newcomer—it would be interesting to find out how 'adventurous' water snails are in trying out new additions to their diet.

Distribution maps of 1. Hydrocharis morsus-ranae *(Frog-bit)*; 2. Callitriche spp *(Starwort)*; 3. Elodea canadensis *(Canadian Pondweed)*; 4. Phragmites communis *(Reed)*.

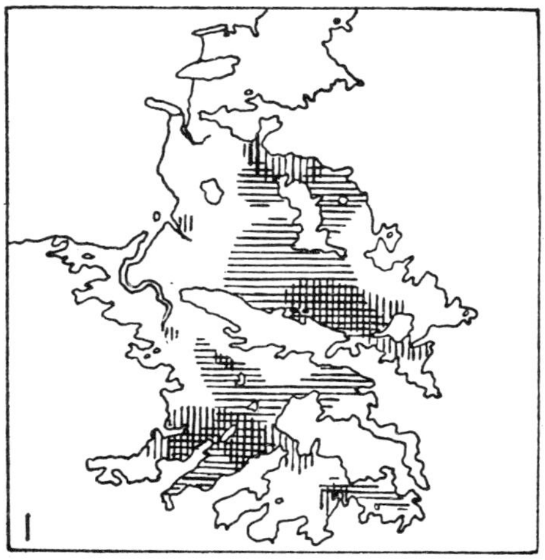

Following the aquatic plants, it is the turn of the 'reeds' to become established, as the ditch cycle moves on. The two Reed-grasses and the true Reed are plants which thrive with 'their feet in the water'. They are all strikingly tall and soon form the dominant form of vegetation. It is this group which has given us the term 'reed-swamp association'.

REED-GRASS (*Phalaris arundinacea*) is usually the first of this trio to occur in any quantity. Like the others, it grows up to some six feet in height. However, its flower head is fairly compact and much less branched than either of the other two species. Its importance lies in the fact that its dead leaves persist throughout the winter and help considerably to build up the organic content of the ditches. At the same time its creeping rootstock extends outwards, consolidating the soft soil and making it firmer. It is at its best in June/July when the pale green leaves set off the purplish tinge of the flower head.

REED-GRASS (*Glyceria maxima*) carries the loosest flower head of the three reeds. It flowers in July/August producing lovely yellow-brown spikelets above broad bright green leaves. It rarely forms such extensive beds as does the true Reed but occasionally it is plentiful enough to be worth cutting for winter fodder. Like the other Reed-grass, it grows from a creeping rootstock and plays a similar part in the succession. A close relative, Flote Grass (*G. fluitans*) occurs quite frequently but it has a very different form. The stems are very weak and, as a result, the plant is usually to be seen sprawling out from the side of the ditch, the leaves often floating on the surface of the water. The other two species of Flote Grass (*G. declimata* and *G. plicata*) are much more restricted (or, since grasses are not usually popular objects of study, it may be that they are less frequently identified and recorded).

REED (*Phragmites communis*) grows somewhere at the side of

almost every ditch and in late August its purple flower heads are carried 8ft or more above the water level. Although the reeds are sometimes flattened when cattle drink from the ditch, they are not grazed and, since they can thrive in conditions varying from marsh to aquatic, their main enemy is themselves. They produce a very large quantity of litter which tends to make the ground too dry for them. Although there are still a few thatched cottages on the Levels, these reeds are seldom cut for thatching.

BUR-REEDS (*Sparganium* spp). The plants in this group throw up a flowering spike with male flowers at the tip. Typically they carry some four or five male flowers, each looking like a rounded catkin. Below these are the globular female flowers; before they are fertilised these are black with silvery stigmas. At this stage, the whole plant looks like a green candelabra with the yellow male flowers looking like glowing candles and the female flowers adding a sophisticated decoration. Three of the four British species can be found on Sedgemoor, and the Branched Bur-reed (*S. ramosum*) is quite common. As its name implies, this species has the candelabra-type flowering spike, but the Small Bur-reed (*S. simplex*) has its flowers on an unbranched stem. Although this is the rarer of the two species, it is quite widespread and can be found spasmodically over the whole of the area south of Wedmore. The third British species, Least Bur-reed (*S. minimum*), can be found in only three stations in the south of England. One of these is near Walton on the peat moors, where random digging for peat has left small water-filled pits in the ground. Its survival here is very problematical, as the pits are being filled in with litter and becoming less suitable as a habitat. Unfortunately, it is difficult to take steps to protect the plant as this area is outside the control of the Nature Conservancy (now a Local Nature Reserve).

RUSHES (*Juncus* spp) can usually be distinguished from the other long thin-leaved monocotyledons since their stems are cylindrical and the flowers form in a brown cluster along the stem. The leaves are sheathing so that they too appear cylindrical. Nine species of Rush occur on the Levels proper and a further species, Sea Rush (*J. maritimus*), occurs near the mouth of the River Parrett. Amongst those commonly occurring is Slender Rush (*J. effusus*); when Gilbert White wrote to a friend of his in 1775 he described it as 'the proper species for this [use in a rush light] purpose. One rush burnt for one hour and a quarter'. When required for a floor covering, however, there was less selectivity in the choice of rushes; whichever species was nearest to hand appears to have been used.

SEDGES (*Carex* spp) form the dominant vegetation in the older ditches. Some thirty-three different species have been recorded from the Levels (excluding the maritime strip), though three of these have not been found recently. Lesser Fox Sedge (*Carex diandra*) was last recorded near Shapwick in 1906. Divided Sedge (*C. divisa*) is still to be found near the coast and on the off-shore

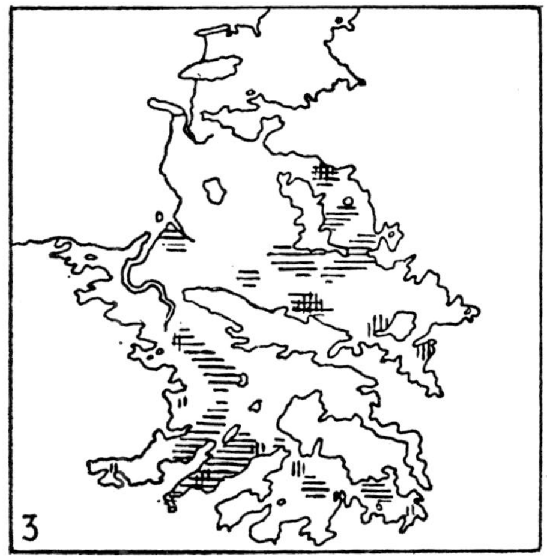

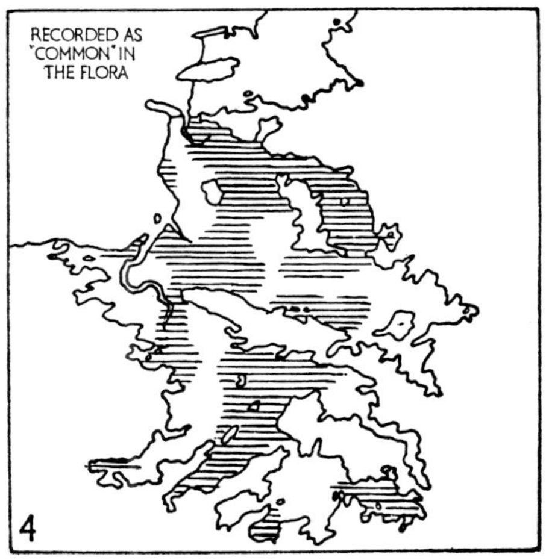

RECORDED IN THE COUNTY FLORA 1898, AND SUPPLEMENT, 1914

RECORDED DURING 1955-65

island of Steep Holm, but it seems extinct at its old station near Burtle. Tawny Sedge (*C. hostiana*) is classed as not uncommon for Britain, but its 'liking' for acidic conditions has led to its extinction and no records have been obtained since the 1920s. Of the species still present, Pond Sedge (*C. riparia*) and (*C. acutiformis*) are the commonest. They can be found at the side of almost every ditch; in late April and early May they make an attractive show of colour with bright yellow anthers above blackish-brown female glumes, the whole carried above pale green leaves. Tussock Sedge (*C. paniculata*) is confined to the peat moors (see p 119), but the other large sedge, Drooping Sedge (*C. pendula*), occurs as a gracefully arched plant in woodland shade. The small Brown Sedge (*C. distica*) often tinges a particularly low-lying field with its pale leaves and warm brown flower spikes. It often grows with the Green-winged Orchid (*Orchis morio*), its foliage making an attractive background for the purple orchids. The remaining sedges all occur on the peat moors and a dozen or so are also quite widely distributed throughout the Levels.

Distribution maps of 1. Sparganium ramosum *(Branched Bur-Reed)*; 2. Filipendula ulmaria *(Meadow-Sweet)*; 3. Iris pseudocorus *(Yellow Flag)*; 4. Rumex hydrolapathum *(Great Water Dock)*.

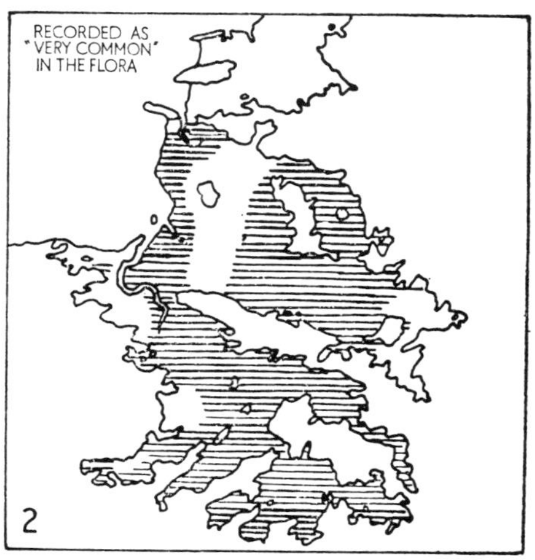

MEADOW-SWEET (*Filipendula ulmaria*) is not the dominant plant on Sedgemoor but on a late-June evening its scent completely fills the air; the showy, creamy-white plumes of flowers stand out in the fading light and every breath becomes a pleasure. Its two local names, Honeysweet and Queen of the Meadow, are as delightful as the plant. When it grows with the deep blue flowers of Tufted Vetch rambling amongst it, it makes a most attractive picture.

MARSH BEDSTRAW (*Galium palustre*) is a secondary plant in this community; it can only grow well once the primary supporting plants are established. Its stems appear above the water surface in April and these weak trailing aerial shoots obtain support from sedges and rushes growing in the vicinity. Like its hedgerow relative, Goosegrass (*G. aparine*), its capacity to 'lean on' its neighbours is very well developed; during July it often appears to be the dominant ditch plant, since its white starry flowers often hide the supporting vegetation. Fen Bedstraw (*G. uliginosum*) is rarely found except on the peat moors around Shapwick.

YELLOW FLAG (*Iris pseudacorus*) adds to the cream and yellow which are by far the commonest flower colours on Sedgemoor in the early part of the year; this colour pattern seems to reach a climax when the Iris blooms in late May. It occurs all over the Levels, usually growing at the sides of ditches, and is particularly plentiful south of the Polden Hills. The glorious yellow flowers make the ditch edges comparable with many herbaceous borders.

BITTERSWEET or WOODY NIGHTSHADE (*Solanum dulcamara*) is a weak straggling shrub rather than a true herbaceous plant. Darwin very accurately described it as 'one of the feeblest and poorest of twiners'; nowadays it could aptly be called a 'layabout'. Though its stem does make a few twists and turns as it uses other material for support, the only accurate description of it is the schoolmaster's

*The distinctive very large leaves of the Great Water Dock (*Rumex hydrolapathum*).*

hackneyed comment 'could do better if it tried'. This even applies to the flowers, which are about the size and shape of a potato flower; but the colour of the outer corolla lobes is a glorious royal purple which offsets the central ring of yellow anthers. Surely, one feels, if the plant is going to have these rich purple and gold trappings, it might hold them up a bit more and make them a bit larger. However, the success of the plant shows that its size and pattern have evolved because of their survival value and should be appreciated as such.

DOCK (*Rumex* spp) has two species which occur in this marshy ditch-side habitat. Great Water Dock (*Rumex hydrolapathum*), common along the edge of the ditches, lives up to its name with its 6ft tall flowering spikes. The leaves are equally large in proportion, but when they emerge in spring they are rolled in along the line of the mid-rib, which gives them a spear-shaped appearance. They are adapted to pierce through any surrounding vegetation before they open out, so that the lamina may get as much light as possible. Marsh Dock (*R. palustris*) has not been noted for several years; even forty years ago it was described as very rare, being recorded from only five stations. It has certainly disappeared from two of these and can probably be included among those plants which have completely vanished from the Levels.

LESSER WATER PARSNIP (*Berula erecta*) is still quite common and will sometimes dominate a stretch of rhyne. On the other hand, Greater Water Parsnip (*Sium latifolia*) was described as rare some fifty years ago and has probably become even rarer. This is a pity since the species is becoming increasingly rare in southern England and the Levels are its last remaining habitat in the west of the country.

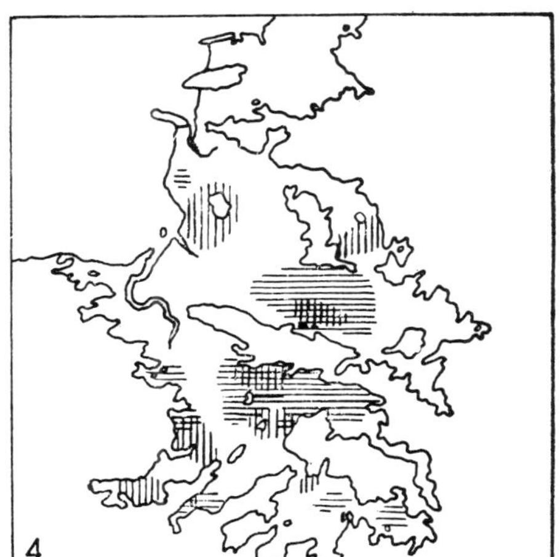

RECORDED IN THE COUNTY FLORA 1898, AND SUPPLEMENT, 1914

RECORDED DURING 1955-65

The following table shows those plants which occur less frequently, though they are still quite common and easily found on the moors.

PLANTS RECORDED LESS THAN TWENTY TIMES		AGE OF THE DITCHES Newly cleaned	Recently cleaned	Middle-aged	Old
Azolla filiculoides	Water Fern	8	4	5	0
Wolffia arrhiza	Least Duckweed	3	0	0	0
Characeae	Stoneworts	10	8	0	0
Ceratophyllum demersum	Hornwort	9	15	0	0
Utricularia vulgaris	Bladderwort	3	8	0	0
Potamogeton spp	Pondweeds		13		
Ranunculus aquatilis	Water Crowfoot	2	7	0	0
Hottonia palustris	Water Violet	2	15	0	0
Polygonum amphibium	Amphibious Bistort	7	2	0	0
Alisma plantago-aquatica	Water Plantain	3	3	13	4
Sagittaria sagittifolia	Arrow-head	3	9	0	0
Oenanthe spp	Water Dropwort	2	1	1	1
Veronica anagallis-aquatica	Water Speedwell	1	3	0	0
Apium nodiflorum	Fool's Watercress	0	1	6	1
Nasturtium officinale	Watercress	2	2	3	0
Ranunculus sceleratus	Celery-leaved Buttercup	1	1	6	0
Veronica beccabunga	Brooklime	0	1	0	0
Lysimachia nummularia	Creeping Jenny	3	6	4	2
Mentha aquatica	Water Mint	1	5	9	12
Equisetum spp	Horsetails	0	0	0	10
Hydrocotyle vulgaris	Pennywort	0	1	0	0
Caltha palustris	Marsh Marigold	0	1	1	0
Polygonum hydropiper	Water-pepper	0	0	2	0
Butomus umbellatus	Flowering Rush	0	0	1	0
Scrophularia aquatica	Water Figwort	0	0	1	0
Dipsacus fullonum	Teasel	0	1	0	0
Thalictrum flavum	Meadow Rue	0	1	1	0
Lysimachia vulgaris	Yellow Loosestrife	0	2	1	0
Lythrum salicaria	Purple Loosestrife	0	2	3	5
Hypericum tetrapterum	Square-stemmed St John's Wort	0	1	1	0
Scutellaria galericulata	Skullcap	0	1	1	0
Angelica sylvestris	Wild Angelica	0	1	5	1
Pulicaria dysenterica	Fleabane	1	9	5	5
Symphytum officinale	Comfrey	2	1	0	0
Myosotis palustris	Water Forget-me-not	0	0	0	7
Typha latifolia	Reedmace	0	2	10	15
Cirsium palustre	Marsh Thistle	0	1	0	1
Epilobium hirsutum	Codlins and Cream	0	3	0	7
Salix spp	Willow	0	3	3	1
Alnus glutinosa	Alder	0	1	1	4
Crataegus monogyna	Hawthorn	0	1	0	2
Rubus spp	Blackberry	0	5	2	7

Because this table indicates those plants which occur less frequently, it must be realised that the figures are less reliable. If the figure for Duckweed varied by ten it would make very little difference to the pattern; but a difference of even one applied to some of the plants in this table would apparently either double their population or lead to their exclusion from the table. By chance, some plants which occur fairly frequently do not appear in the tables whilst others, such as Skullcap, are given undue prominence. I have listed them according to their sequence in the succession, based on my general observations rather than on the numerical values; and in describing them I have been selective.

WATER FERN (*Azolla filiculoides*) is another introduced plant; first recorded in England in 1910, within three years it spread through the southern counties. It is less hardy than the Duckweeds and, after a severe winter, quite rare; for this reason it is generally limited in its distribution to the south of England. This little floating fern looks more like a moss than a conventional fern. It has minute two-lobed leaves which overlap each other along the small branched stems. The individual stems are usually less than an inch in length, but once established it grows so well that it can become the dominant floating plant. In the early part of the year, it has an attractive silvery-green sheen and in autumn turns to brick red. It grew particularly well in 1969 and 1970, and appears to be increasing; some ditches were completely covered by it.

LEAST DUCKWEED (*Wolffia arrhiza*) has the distinction of being the smallest British flowering plant. If it is growing abundantly, it looks as if the water surface has been dusted with golden green grains of pearl barley. When other Duckweeds are present, it can best be identified by rubbing a mass of them between the fingers. If Least Duckweed is present it has a gritty feeling and a close examination reveals that the egg-shaped fronds are rootless. Although it can produce flowers, these have not been recorded in England; the plant is quite rare, being recorded only in south-east England, part of Wales and Somerset.

STONEWORTS (*Characeae*) are closely related to the Blanket Weeds, but, unlike them, they are differentiated into a main shoot with whorls of short cylindrical branches. They also differ in that they are submerged aquatics, growing upright from a branching rhizome-like structure. Their reproduction is complicated yet basically primitive. The lateral branches have pinhead-sized swellings along them, which are the egg-cells and sperm sacs. The sperms eventually swim freely in the water to bring about fertilisation. The mature plants are usually pale green and somewhat straggly and fragile in appearance; yet this apparent fragility is deceptive for they can hold their own against much tougher-looking competitors. Four species of *Chara*, two of *Tolypella* and one of *Nitella* have all been found on the Levels, as has the Willow Moss (*Fontinalis antipyretica*).

HORNWORT (*Ceratophyllum demersum*) and the Water Milfoils (*Myriophyllum* spp) are all found in the rhynes, especially south of the Polden Hills. Spineless Hornwort (*Ceratophyllum submersum*) was recorded near Glastonbury in 1726 but there are no recent records and it must now be considered extinct on the Levels. The Common Hornwort feels rather rough to the touch; large amounts of it are eaten by young roach, the stomachs of some fish being almost full of it. All three species of Milfoil (*Myriophyllum spicatum, M. verticillatum* and *M. alterniflorum*) occur on the Levels, but only the spiked form (*M. spicatum*) occurs at all plentifully.

BLADDERWORT (*Utricularia vulgaris*) is a floating, not a rooted, aquatic plant. The flowers are a lovely deep yellow borne on deep red stems, a very attractive plant indeed. Their submerged leaves are particularly worth examination. As with many water plants, these leaves are finely divided so that the whole stem looks rather like a worn bottle-brush. Attached to these filamentous leaves are the bladders which give the plant its name. In the common species the bladder may be up to 4mm across. Its function is to trap insects and other small creatures; it has been described as the most advanced and complex form of trap found in the plant kingdom. In the 'set' condition, the walls of the trap are slightly concave and under tension. A door acts as a valve and prevents the entry of water. This door also has an outer funnel of trigger hairs. When a small water animal blunders against these hairs, the door opens, the walls expand rapidly and water is sucked into the bladder. This water current carries the prey with it. The door then closes and the bladder eventually reverts to the 'set' state. The walls of the bladder are lined with small hairs, which some authorities suggest are associated with digestion. Others believe that there is no active digestion on the part of the plant and that probably the prey decays due to bacterial action. The decomposition products are eventually absorbed, so adding to the nitrogen intake of the plant. All four members of this family (*U. vulgaris, neglecta, intermedia* and *minor*) almost certainly grew on the Levels in the past. Nowadays only the Common Bladderwort (*U. vulgaris*) and the Lesser Bladderwort (*U. minor*) can be found; the other two species must be considered casualties in the battle for survival.* Common Bladderwort lives up to its name and is much the commoner of the two. It grows, sometimes in great profusion, on King's Sedgemoor, Butleigh Moor, Westhay Moor and Shapwick Heath, while the Lesser Bladderwort is now restricted to the non-alkaline ditches of the peat moor around Ashcott. Although Bladderwort is equipped with these special traps, it can thrive quite well without preying on animals. Strasburger, writing in 1898, says 'in one bladder as many as ten or twelve crustaceans will often be found imprisoned at the same time'. Specimens collected recently, when crustacea were active in the water, showed that out of three thousand bladders examined by hand lens, only one per cent contained animals, or animal remains. In a laboratory, the plants continued to grow in ditch water which had been filtered to exclude any water creatures (minute creatures could have got through the filter, but checks on the water showed no creature large enough to be seen with a × 10 hand lens). The distribution of the Bladderworts does show a

*The underwater stems, leaves and bladders of Bladderwort (*Utricularia vulgaris*). The bladders act like miniature lobster traps to capture small water creatures.*

*The action of the insect-trapping Bladderwort (*Utricularia spp*).*

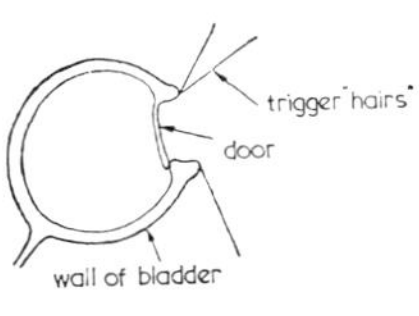

The prey touches the outer trigger hairs

The walls expand, the door begins to open and the prey is drawn in with the inrush of water

The door is fully opened and the prey is inside the bladder

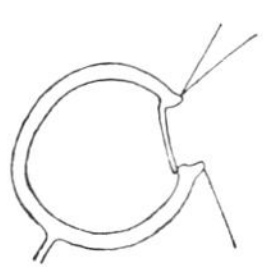

The door closes thus holding the prey and resetting the trap

* *U. neglecta* has now been rediscovered.

definite reduction in its area. The Lesser Bladderwort is certainly affected by the restriction of the acidic peat, and with the general trend to alkaline conditions it will probably become extinct. The Common Bladderwort seems less dependent on acidic conditions and grows well at pH 7·5 (slightly alkaline). It does, however, grow best in deep water and it may well be the absence of this habitat which is limiting its range.

PONDWEEDS (*Potamogeton* spp) are a frequently ignored group. Canadian Pondweed is well known to any one who has kept an aquarium, but the native species are rarely mentioned. Of the eleven species which occur on Sedgemoor, Shining Pondweed (*P. lucens*) and Opposite-leaved Pondweed (*P. densus*) are the most common. In most species the small green flowers are carried above the water surface, but in Opposite-leaved Pondweed even these are submerged. Broad-leaved Pondweed (*P. natans*) is the exception in that it has a number of oval-shaped floating leaves which turn a rich orange-brown very early in the year. Since most of the Pondweeds are dark green, some stretches of ditch look extremely attractive with the orange-brown of Broad-leaved Pondweed and the pale green of Starwort showing against the deep green backcloth of the other Pondweeds.

WATER CROWFOOT (*Ranunculus aquatilis*) is not really one plant but a convenient name used to cover a closely related group which is now divided into eight species and a number of sub-species. However, three main divisions can be recognised, ie those plants whose leaves are entirely submerged and finely dissected; those whose leaves are floating and more or less entire, and those plants with both submerged dissected leaves and entire floating ones. Three species are common on the Levels: *Ranunculus aquatilis*, with both floating and submerged leaves, occurs in many of the ditches; while *R. circinatus* and *R. trichophyllus*, each with finely divided submerged leaves, can also be found occasionally. Although *R. hederaceus* and *R. lenormardi* are mentioned as being present in the early part of this century, a survey during the latter part of the 1950s failed to find them, indicating that they are now either extinct on the moors, or extremely scarce.

WATER VIOLET (*Hottonia palustris*) sometimes occurs in great profusion and completely dominates a ditch. It first becomes noticeable in early spring when the bright green whorls of its much divided leaves develop below the surface. By April, the whorls of flowers appear and it is their delicate pale violet petals which give the plant its name. Not only does it look attractive, but it flowers so abundantly that it often scents the air. Apart from Cheddar Moor, where it is unusual nowadays, this plant shows little change in its distribution and its position is much as it was fifty years ago. However, its position in the succession appears very critical since it only grows well in shallow water with a limited amount of shade. Within a season or two it may

*Water Crowfoot (*Ranunculus aquatilis*). The upper photograph shows it completely covering the surface of a ditch. The lower photograph illustrates its ability to survive in dry seasons on the wet mud surface.*

completely disappear as the ditch becomes too overgrown.

WATER-LILIES (*Nymphaea* spp) find few suitable habitats on the Levels. The White Water-lily (*Nymphaea alba*) is growing now in a few pools near Brent Knoll railway station; it was recorded in the same place fifty years ago. It was probably introduced into these pools, but since its pollen has been identified from the lake village site at Glastonbury, it can be considered a true inhabitant of the Levels. The Yellow Water-lily, or Brandy Bottles (*Nuphar lutea*), is commoner but chiefly restricted to the main waterways where there is more suitable depth and a continuous flow of water. Thus it is found in King's Sedgemoor Drain, the River Cary, the River Brue and on the Bridgwater–Taunton Canal. It is surprising that the County Flora does not show this lily as widespread in either the Bridgwater–Taunton Canal or King's Sedgemoor Drain, though it is now very common in both these stretches of water. It is also present in similar waterways in the southern parts of the Levels, such as the upper stretches of the River Parrett and the River Yeo. Although individual flowers of the Yellow Water-lily are quite striking, its rather spasmodic flowering period prevents it from making a display comparable with its white relative.

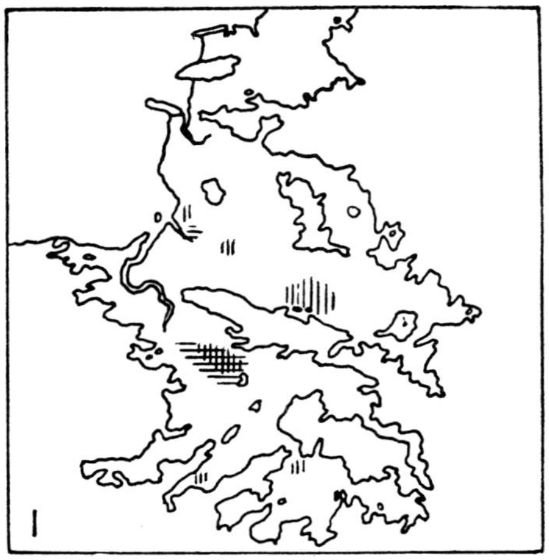

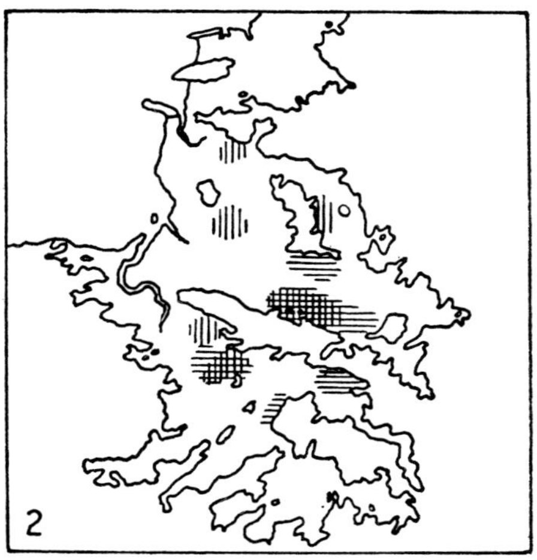

Distribution maps of 1. Ceratophyllum demersum *(Hornwort)*; 2. Utricularia vulgaris *(Bladderwort)*; 3. Hottonia palustris *(Water Violet)*; 4. Hippuris vulgaris *(Marestail)*.

MARESTAIL (*Hippuris vulgaris*) is an odd looking plant which grows in a number of rhynes south of the Poldens and on Westbury Moor. In the early part of the year the plant is totally submerged and consists of a central stem with whorls of leaves arising at intervals. These leaves are thin, strap-shaped and about 3in long; when the stem is 'combed out' by any water current, the plant's name seems most appropriate.The flowers are carried on extensions of the stem which emerge above the water surface. These stems grow vertically out of the water for some 9–12in. Like the submerged stems, the aerial ones bear whorls of leaves but these are shorter and stockier. Since they decrease in length towards the top of the plant, the whole structure has the appearance of a miniature Christmas tree. The plant is not widespread, but is locally abundant.

WATER PLANTAIN (*Alisma plantago-aquatica*) is common in most of the ditches but its stockier relative, ARROW-HEAD (*Sagittaria sagittifolia*), attracts more attention. The flowers of the Water Plantain family are uncommon in that they have only three petals. In Arrow-head the flowers are about an inch across and borne on a spike; they are white with a brownish purple patch at their base. It is the arrowhead-shaped leaves, appearing just above the water surface, which give the plant its name.

SWEET FLAG (*Acorus calamus*) must now be considered extinct on Sedgemoor. It gets the second part of its name from its iris or flag-like leaves. The flowering spike is made up of small, tightly packed green flowers and looks like an elongated young fir cone. Even without the flower, it can be identified by its leaves which have a distinctly crinkly edge. It was found near Wedmore in 1791, but has not been recorded in that area since that date. It also seems to have disappeared, about 1920, from its last two habitats on King's Sedgemoor and the peat moors.

WATER DROPWORTS (*Oenanthe* spp) occur spasmodically across Sedgemoor. Six species are present, including the Fine-leaved species (*O. aquatica*); the Levels mark the limit of its south-western range. Parsley Water Dropwort (*O. pimpinelloides*), apart from a few scattered habitats, is found in a triangle with its base running along the south coast from Torquay to just beyond Portsmouth and with its apex on the Somerset Levels. Both these species tend to grow rather tall and rank, while the Tubular Water Dropwort (*O. fistulosa*) rarely grows more than a foot above the water surface; the petioles as well as the stem are tubular and, in the early stages of growth, look almost rush-like. The Fine-leaved and Parsley forms grow in such a way that the stem (1–2ft tall to the first leaves) is immersed but the leaves are aerial. The Tubular form is a smaller plant; its stem and the petioles which grow obliquely from it are submerged and therefore need the internal air space. River Water Dropwort (*O. fluvialis*) has unfortunately disappeared in the last fifty years. It was recorded from the River Parrett at Langport and the River Cary at Somerton, but now seems to have gone from both these habitats.

WATERCRESS (*Nasturtium officinale*) is quite common near the moorland villages; local legend has it that the plant only grows in the vicinity of sewerage. So firmly fixed is this idea that, if it is pointed out that it grows in a place well away from human habitation, the answer is that there must be an old cesspit nearby, from a house long since pulled down. Fool's Watercress (*Apium nodiflorum*) is found in similar habitat, but Marshwort (*A. inundatum*) has only been recorded at two stations near Westonzoyland and on the peat moors.

CELERY-LEAVED BUTTERCUP (*Ranunculus sceleratus*) is normally found growing on wet mud, but during the winter it may be standing in several inches of water. This plant is spread widely over the area, though it is nowhere plentiful. In slightly drier conditions and where the soil is naturally alkaline the Creeping Buttercup (*R. repens*) usually represents the family. Where the ground is drier still, the Bulbous and Field Buttercup (*R. bulbosus* and *R. acris*) take over. Lesser Spearwort (*R. flammula*) is restricted to the peat moors where the soil is sufficiently acid.

WATER MINT (*Mentha aquatica*) is usually found growing amongst the lower vegetation. Its very strong scent is particularly noticeable when the leaves are crushed; it is often possible to identify it with one's feet when walking over the prostrate stems. The scent is sweeter than that of garden mint but still very characteristic of that family.

HORSETAILS (*Equisetum* spp) are often mentioned as being the

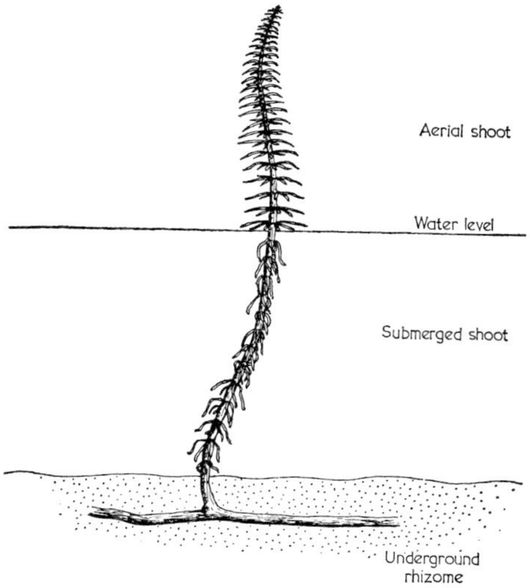

Marestail (Hippuris vulgaris).

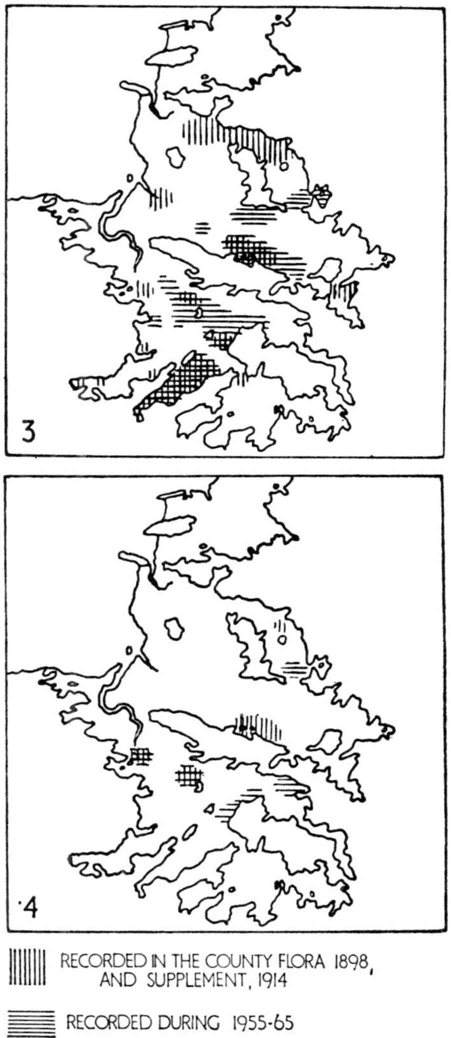

Horsetails emerging in a waterlogged ditch.

A section through the stem of Horsetails. The large air spaces are so that air can pass down to the lower parts of the plant growing in oxygen-low water and mud.

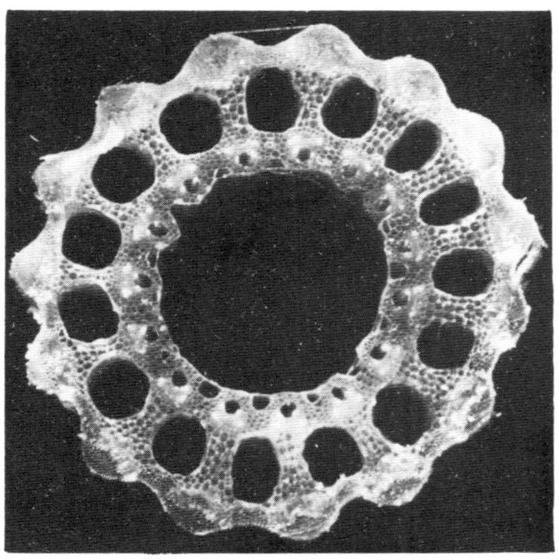

descendants of the flora which earlier gave us our coal measures. Water Horsetail (*E. fluviatile*) and Marsh Horsetail (*E. palustre*) are very common. Unlike the Common Horsetail (*E. arvense*), these two species have few side branches, the Water Horsetail being sometimes completely unbranched, so that it looks very rush-like. Water Horsetail is usually a pale green while Marsh Horsetail is a dark green. A more reliable method of distinguishing them is to gently squeeze the stem: Water Horsetail feels hollow and Marsh Horsetail much more solid (it has only a small central hollow). The attraction of these plants lies in the lower end of each stem section, where there is a most delicate shade of ivory fading into a blush pink which in turn is replaced by the normal green colouring.

FLOWERING RUSH (*Butomus umbellatus*) is one of the most showy monocotyledons. It gets its name from the rush-like stem, but the flowering head with its umbel of six-petalled flowers shows that this is not a true rush. There are usually twelve to fifteen flowers in the umbel, each about an inch wide and a delicate rose-pink colour. Since the plant is some 3–4ft in height, it well deserves to be called 'one of our handsomest aquatics'.

MARSH MARIGOLD (*Caltha palustris*) is better described by its other name, Kingcup, as it does resemble a king-sized buttercup. It is closely related to the buttercups, but structurally the flower is quite different. The true petals are reduced to a small ridge, while the so-called petals are really sepals, which have taken over the function of advertising the plant to its insect pollinators. This is one of the earliest of the marsh plants to come into flower and it is usually fully out in early April. It is particularly common on West Sedgemoor where whole fields are sometimes covered in its yellow flowers. Elsewhere it is usually restricted to the edges of ditches, and often marks the site of a ditch which has been allowed to 'fill in'.

WILD TEASEL (*Dipsacus fullonum*), one of the two wild species, is still widespread and common along ditch banks and in moist habitats. The Small Teasel or Shepherd's Rod (*D. pilosus*) has never been common but can still be found near Ashcott and Taunton. The commercial growing of teasels is dealt with in Chapter Nine.

CREEPING JENNY (*Lysimachia nummularia*) and YELLOW LOOSESTRIFE (*L. vulgaris*) are both members of the primrose family. Creeping Jenny is a low-growing plant, putting out horizontal stems with opposite leaves which are roughly the size and shape of a shilling. This leaf pattern gives it the alternative name of Moneywort. It will tolerate a fairly high light intensity (it is often grown on rockeries), but usually does best on the north-facing ditch banks, where its stems form a prostrate mat. The flowers, a buttercup yellow, are about as large as the leaves and carried on very short stalks. The flowers of Yellow Loosestrife are very similar but carried in panicles on stems 3–4ft high; in good growing conditions the plant can reach 6ft.

PURPLE LOOSESTRIFE (*Lythrum salicaria*) flowers at the same time as Yellow Loosestrife and often intermingles with it at the edge of ditches. This plant carries spikes of brilliant purple flowers, so that when the two do occur together the effect is very striking. These two species are not related; it is their general rather than botanical similarity which has led to them sharing a common name. As the distribution map shows, this plant has altered its spread very considerably during the last forty years. In the County Flora, it was recorded as being particularly common on the moor immediately south of the Mendips and on Shapwick Heath. Small patches of it occurred elsewhere but it was relatively scarce south of the Polden Hills. Since it is such a showy plant, it is most unlikely that the recorders missed it. In my own more recent survey I found that the pattern of its distribution was an almost complete inversion of the earlier picture. South of the Mendips it is relatively scarce, while on the Levels south of the Poldens it can be seen on the banks of almost every ditch. It is still common on Shapwick Heath but has extended its territory and is now widespread over much of Mark Moor. One can only suppose that some critical factor relating to drainage, and affecting the amount of water in the soil, has been responsible for this striking change in its distribution.

FLEABANE (*Pulicaria dysenterica*), one of the commonest of the compositae or daisy family, does particularly well where the silt is so fine that it is bordering on being a clay, and the ground is almost permanently waterlogged. The flowers are of the daisy type, all yellow, and about one inch across. The fine hairs on the leaves give them a silver-green appearance; in some plants this can be quite attractive but in Fleabane it simply looks as if the plant has been attacked by mildew. Although its flowers follow the same basic pattern as Fleabane, Marsh Ragwort (*Senecio aquaticus*) looks far more delicate. The ray petals are more spaced

Teasels have, for many years, been grown in the area. They are used to raise the nap on woollen cloth.

out than those of Common Ragwort (*S. jacobaea*) and the plant is neither as tall nor as coarse growing as its wayside relative.

REEDMACE OR FALSE BULRUSH (*Typha latifolia*), locally called Cat's Tail, is the plant commonly depicted in the story of Moses and the Bulrushes. It looks more exotic and 'eastern' than the true Bulrushes, which are grass-like. There are some very fine stands of it to be found on the peat moors; elsewhere it occurs in small clumps at the edge of ditches. The velvety, dark brown heads are often used in flower arrangements. The Lesser Reedmace (*T. angustifolia*) is far less common but well established in three stations: one near Bridgwater, one on the peat moors and one near Berrow.

MARSH THISTLE (*Cirsium palustre*) has purple-red flowers and is one of the tallest herbaceous plants on the Levels. Commonly growing 5–6ft tall, if the plant is partly sheltered by reeds or other tallish vegetation, it can reach 8ft and more. Although this thistle is very widespread, it does not grow in the clumps that are associated with the Common Field Thistle. The unbranched spikes of Marsh Thistle often mark the edge of a ditch like untidily placed stakes. While Marsh Thistle is a tall, very spiky plant, Meadow Thistle (*C. dissectum*) is a short, softer relation. On the Levels its appearance is spasmodic, being more or less restricted to the less alkaline areas and growing in even wetter ground than Marsh Thistle will normally tolerate. When it does occur, it is often quite numerous and a field can be studded with its soft lilac-coloured flowers.

CODLINS AND CREAM (*Epilobium hirsutum*) is also known as Great Willow-herb. It has reddish flowers with a cream centre; as codlins are small red apples, its first name seems particularly appropriate in an apple-growing county. From July onwards, this plant grows with the reeds and adds colour to the hedge of tall ditch-side plants. Occasionally Tufted Vetch (*Vicia cracca*) grows with the Codlins and Cream; its blue flowers hanging in clusters below the pink and white stars make a very pleasing picture.

Distribution maps of 1. Cardamine pratensis *(Milkmaids)*; 2. Primula veris *(Cowslip)*; 3. Primula vulgaris *(Primrose)*; 4. Eriophorum angustifolium *(Cotton-grass)*.

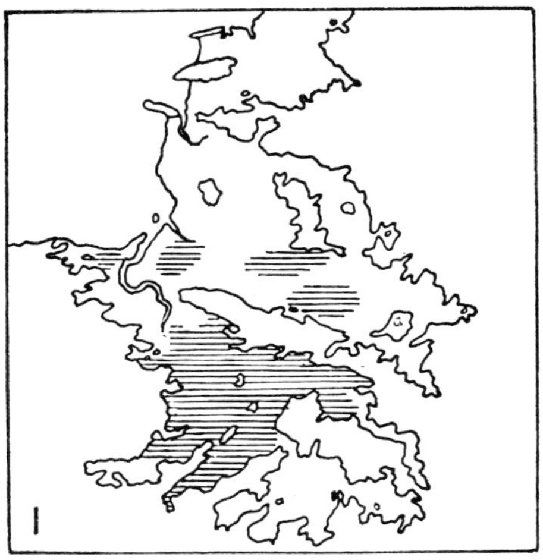

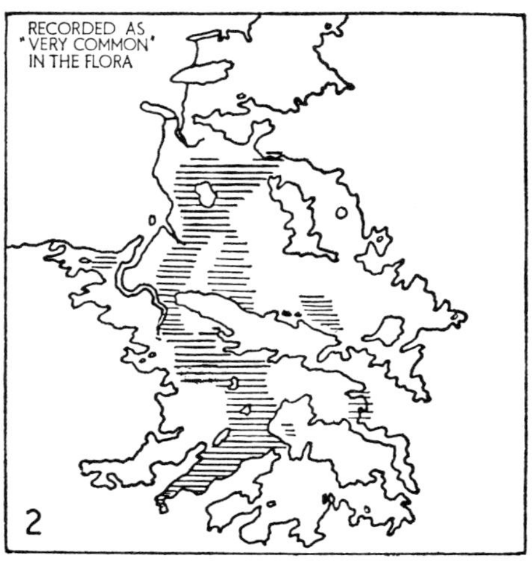

The plants of the meadows

Many of the plants of the ditches spill over into the fields—or so it seems; in practice it is the reverse which has happened. Here and there on the Levels it is possible to find fields which have been 'unimproved'. Sometimes these fields occur in blocks covering several hundred acres, such as on West Sedgemoor and on the Tealham/Tadham Moors; in other places there may be just a few fields in isolation. Depending on the criteria of the observer, these fields can be said to cover some five to ten percent of the total area of the Levels. Put the other way round, some 90–95% of our fields have undergone some form of agricultural improvement, particularly since the last war.

A close inspection of these fields shows that many of the 'ditch bank' plants grow across the whole width of the field. A field which is destined for hay will carry a flora of early flowering plants, Meadow-Sweet, Yellow Flag, Marsh Orchid, Yellow Rattle, Ragged Robin and Cowslips are just a few of the 50 or so species which can be found; whilst a field which is grazed will carry the ground hugging species such as Creeping Jenny and Bugle and the 'grazing resisters' such as Marsh Thistle.

As the farmers are put under increasing pressure to intensify, so these plants are pushed out from the main part of the field until their only home is the ditchbank. The plants do not spill over from the ditch into the field, they are being squeezed out of the fields into the ditches.

Without doubt, the grasses and closely related groups are the dominant plants at all times. Unfortunately they are often difficult, if not impossible, to identify when they are not in flower and this makes accurate counting a rather pointless occupation. In general the visitor sees the grasses as a green blanket against which the more brightly coloured flowers are displayed. Many of the components of this green backcloth are not true grasses but are either sedges—after all, the area is called Sedgemoor—or the rush-like sedges which include such genera as Spike-rush (*Eleocharis* spp), Club-rush (*Scirpus* spp) and Beak-sedge (*Rhyncospora* spp). Some species, such as Common Spike-rush (*Eleocharis palustris*), are very common and widespread, while others, such as White Beak-sedge (*Rhyncospora alba*), are limited to a few stations near Shapwick on the more acid part of the peat moors. Soil pH is the controlling factor for most of the species in this group, which can be divided into those plants growing in acidic soils and found only on the peat moors, and those plants tolerant of the more alkaline soils and more widely spread over the sedge moors.

This dependence on soil pH is so critical that these plants can easily be used as soil indicators. Of all the rush-like sedges, the Cotton-grass (*Eriophorum angustifolium*) is perhaps the most useful.

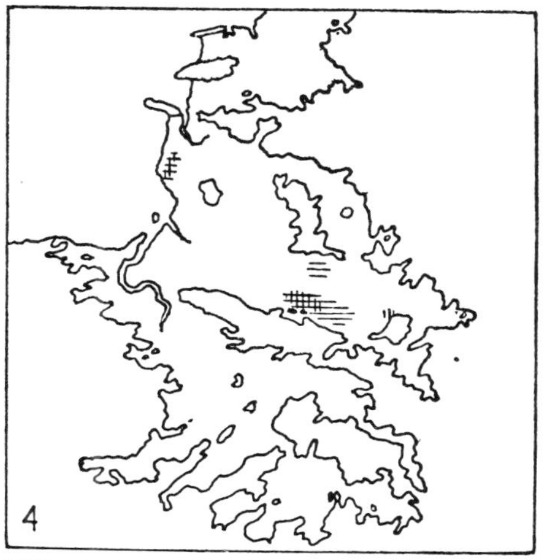

RECORDED IN THE COUNTY FLORA 1898, AND SUPPLEMENT, 1914

RECORDED DURING 1955-65

Cotton Grass. This is one of the plants which colonised the moor at an early stage. Remains of Cotton Grass can easily be identified in the peat today.

*Comfrey (*Symphytum officinale*) can often be seen on the ditch banks. It can be used to make a herbal tea.*

Its cotton-like heads are unmistakable and in July they whiten whole patches of the peat moors. Its only other station on the Levels is near the coast at Berrow where it is found amongst the dunes. Sheathing Cotton-grass or Harestail (*E. vaginatum*) also occurred on the peat moors but has not been recorded there recently.* Fortunately, it can still be found on the Mendips. A third species, Broad-leaved Cotton-grass (*E. latifolium*), does occur in Somerset and has been noted from slightly alkaline or base rich soils. The fact that it has not been recorded from the Levels shows that the use of this group as an indicator of acidic soils is a valid one.

The list of rush-like sedges recorded from the Levels in the County Flora contains six species not on record since 1960. One of these, Sedge (*Cladium mariscus*), is well known from East Anglia though it is becoming rare in the rest of the country; in Norfolk it is usually considered to be the best material for thatching. On Sedgemoor, the Common Reed (*Phragmites communis*) has been used for this purpose, though thatching is uncommon on cottages in the region. Sedge managed to 'hang on' on the Levels until very recently. At the beginning of the century it was known from three stations, King's Sedgemoor, Glastonbury Moor and the Burtle–Catcott Moor; but there have been no records of it during the last four years from any of these stations and it must now be considered extinct on the moors.

In describing the flowering plants of the fields I have selected a few which add much to the fascination and attraction of Sedgemoor.

MILKMAIDS (*Cardamine pratensis*) are so called because the delicate pink colour is said to resemble milkmaids' complexions. The alternative name, Cuckoo Flower, is chosen because it usually flowers in April when the cuckoos are heard. For Sedgemoor it might well be called a rainbow flower, not because of its petal colour but owing to the fact that its burst of pink, covering the whole moor, is a sign that the winter flood water has subsided and the soil is sufficiently dry and aerated to begin the new spring growth.

COWSLIPS (*Primula veris*) flower at about the same time but usually on very slightly drier ground. If the occurrence of the Cowslip and the Primrose (*P. vulgaris*) are mapped separately, the edges of the two maps fit together almost exactly, the boundary between them coinciding with the edge of the Levels. Since many species of primula grow well in gardens and the wild primrose can be easily established, this natural dividing line between the two wild forms emphasises how critical are the factors controlling their occurrence in nature.

RAGGED ROBIN (*Lychnis flos-cuculi*) is one of the few Sedgemoor plants to approach a true red. The floral structure shows its relationship to the Red Campion of the hedgerows, but the petals are so divided that they appear rather untidy and ragged. It can

* Harestail has recently been refound.

often be found at the edge of a ditch, particularly where cattle have pounded the bank as they go to drink. Elsewhere, it follows the pattern imposed by the previous year's flooding.

YELLOW RATTLE (*Rhinanthus minor*). As its name implies, this plant has a yellow flower but it also has a calyx which becomes pale yellow especially as it ripens. The calyx holds the fruit and the seeds and when they are ripe the seeds become loose. These then rattle inside the dry case and give it the second half of its name. Like any normal plant it has leaves which manufacture food but it supplements its diet by stealing from its neighbours. It is a semi-parasite. Side roots are put out by the parent plant and these, through special organs called haustoria, are able to invade the vascular tissue of host plants and draw sustenance from them. Clovers and vetches are frequently used as host plants on the Sedgemoor fields.

ORCHIDS (*Orchis* spp) are found all over the Levels; occasionally some of the fields on Sedgemoor are purple with Green-winged Orchids (*O. morio*) and Marsh Orchids (*O. praetermissa*), but the peat moors produce the widest variety and rarest species.

Once a ditch becomes grown over, it ceases to be a barrier to cattle. Sometimes it is more convenient for a farmer to put a post-and-wire fence along a ditch than to clean it out. The wire prohibits grazing at the ditch edge and permits seedlings of Alder (*Alnus glutinosa*), Willow (usually *Salix fragilis*) and Hawthorn (*Crataegus monogyna*) to become established. Seedlings may also be protected by growing in the middle of a clump of plants which are ignored by cattle. In a few cases, the seedlings are close enough together to form a rough hedge; but more usually they give rise to isolated bushes. When the ditches are eventually cleaned, these small bushes are often grubbed out, but occasionally a few are left to form small trees which in turn produce more seeds to continue the cycle. Apart from these random survivals, willows were encouraged and sometimes planted to line the edges of the ditches. These trees were pollarded to produce a crop of branches, but this practice is declining rapidly. The tops of these pollarded willows often become hollow and fill with leaf litter. A soil forms in them, which supports a variety of plants from nettles to dog roses and ferns. Because they interfere with mechanical ditch-clearing, there are fewer old trees; but there may be more young saplings, because they grow well up on the ditch bank, bend and bow to the grab, and spring back afterwards.

Sedgemoor's fenny fields are changing. Ditches are sometimes allowed to silt up so that fields are converted into larger units and attempts are made to plough the land and change from dairy to arable farming. The ground is still very wet and plant growth is slow in spring. However, there is pressure on the River Authority to improve the drainage still further so that arable farming can become a practical proposition. It is inevitable that this will further affect the plant life of the fens.

The early catkins of Sallow (Salix atrocinerea) *are very welcome to insects.*

5
Plant Life of the Peat Moors

Crossing from the fenny part of Sedgemoor to the peat bog area a distinct change is noticeable. By coincidence, a drove on the edge of Shapwick Heath runs along this dividing line. On the south side, there are fields and ditches, and grazing cattle. There is a scattering of trees, with farmhouses on the slightly higher ground leading up to the Poldens. This typical Sedgemoor fen pattern continues up to include the southern ditch.

On the other side, the picture changes dramatically. The ditch in the foreground supports a different vegetation, and behind this is an area of very rough grazing, studded with Tussock Sedge, Bog Myrtle bushes and alder–willow carr. Immediately behind the carr and filling most of the skyline are the older trees, including oak and pine. Some parts of Shapwick Heath resemble a woodland of smallish trees; there are no forest giants. Instead, there are pools scattered over the whole floor of this woodland, leaving only a narrow, slightly raised path. Some of the pools are open water, others are filled with bright green sphagnum moss; everywhere there is a covering of lichens and the sound of insects. Occasionally there are patches of rough grazing which support very specialised plants. And, notably in two very large areas, the woodland gives way to peat workings. While most of Sedgemoor gives a feeling of oldness, it is oldness within historical times. By contrast, Shapwick Heath conveys an atmosphere not only prehistoric but pre-human. It is not true, but one feels that some parts of the Heath have never been trodden by man.

An analysis of this area shows that the same general pattern of succession takes place but the component parts are different. Some plants occur throughout the whole of the Levels, but a number are either limited to the peat moor or common on the peat and less so outside them.

A species of plant may grow on acid soils because it is especially adapted to do so, or it may grow there because, although it can grow on a variety of soils, its natural competitors do not succeed in acid conditions and therefore cannot suppress it. Thus some species, such as Common Sundew (*Drosera rotundifolia*), are so well adapted to acid conditions that they cannot thrive anywhere else. Others, such as Marsh Pennywort (*Hydrocotyle vulgaris*), can grow in both bog and fen, but are normally suppressed on the alkaline soil by their competitors and therefore more usually found on acid soils.

On the peat soils, nitrogen is often at a premium. Because of the acid conditions, normal breakdown of organic material is interrupted and the nitrogen is either leached out or locked in the debris and not released for further use. This means that plants which can in some way obtain a supply of nitrogen are the ones most likely to be found on peat soil. Some plants, like sphagnum moss, survive because they demand very little nitrogen intake, but a number of other plants have adopted more unusual methods. The Leguminoseae, such as the Birdsfoot-trefoil (*Lotus corniculatus* and *L. uliginosus*), have small nodules on their roots. Inside these nodules are bacteria which can utilise the nitrogen of the air (air is present in the soil) and build it up into organic form. Clover, which belongs to the same family, also has this capacity to house these symbiotic bacteria.

Other plants, such as Eyebright (*Euphrasia* spp), Lousewort (*Pedicularis sylvatica*) and Yellow Rattle (*Rhinanthus* spp) are semi-parasitic. They produce green leaves which manufacture food in the normal way, but they also have roots which tap other plants, often the Leguminoseae, and 'steal' their supply of nitrogen.

Yet a third group, the Sundews (*Drosera* spp) and Butterworts (*Pinguicula* spp), are insectivorous. The nitrogenous protein of their insect prey is digested by enzymes in much the same series of chemical actions as when one digests a piece of steak. Just as one then converts the steak, or some of it, into one's own body protein, so these plants use the products of digestion to build up their protein.

The aquatic plants, both rooted and floating, are much the same in the two types of succession, but in the acid water fewer species are present. On the peat bogs, Duckweeds account for most of the floating-aquatic population and Bladderwort is relatively more common than in fen conditions.

TUSSOCK SEDGE (*Carex paniculata*) is one of the first large plants to invade the aquatic habitat. It can establish itself in water up to about 1ft deep. By developing new growth on top of the old dead leaves, a tussock of up to 3–4ft high and about 2ft across is formed. These tussocks look like miniature trees, especially when they are affected by scrub burning. The outer loose dead leaves are burned away, leaving a blackened central stem which emphasises the resemblance to a tree trunk. Cattle occasionally feed on the young shoots but this causes only a temporary setback to the plant. One rather specialised use of these plants is that they often act as convenient stepping-stones when one is exploring the heath.

MARSH CINQUEFOIL (*Potentilla palustris*) is occasionally plentiful on some patches of open water. The flowers are a rather unusual

*One small patch on the Peat Moors is dominated by Bog Asphodel (*Narthecium ossifragum*). In early July the carpet of starry yellow flowers is a magnificent sight.*

*Bog Bean (*Menyanthes trifoliata*) grows in a very few peaty pools and gets its name from its leaves which look somewhat like those of Broad Beans.*

The open white petals of the Bog Bean carry these very unusual and attractive fringed petals.

brownish-red colour and the leaves clearly divided into five leaflets. This is a much larger plant than its common relative and its creeping stems can make a sizeable mat. Sometimes the mats are so dense that one can walk on them. Crossing a ditch in this way is a little nerve racking; as the mat bounces on the water surface, it is rather like walking on a trampoline; but, unlike the gymnasium situation, one is never sure that the mat will hold!

BOG BEAN (*Menyanthes tri-foliata*) often grows with Cinquefoil. Its three leaflets are slightly fleshy and a glaucous colour. The flowers, borne in spikes, are most attractive, the inside of the petals being white and the outside pink. The petals have the very unusual characteristic of being fringed.

SUNDEW (*Drosera* spp). The Common or Round-leaved Sundew (*D. rotundifolia*) lives up to its name and is very common indeed. Counts taken at random in one 'field' gave an average of 5·5 plants per square foot. As its name also indicates, the round leaf distinguishes it from the second species to be found, the Long-leaved Sundew (*D. intermedia*). Both these insectivorous plants initially catch their prey by the 'fly-paper' method. The leaves are covered with long reddish hair-like tentacles, which secrete a drop of thick viscous fluid at their tip. These drops glistening in the sunlight give the plant its common name. Insects are attracted to the secretion, probably by its odour, which is said to be fungus-like. They become trapped by the sticky fluid; then the tentacles and the whole leaf blade slowly bend towards the centre so that the leaf forms a tube which is U-shaped in cross section. Roughly along the centre line of the leaf (there is no clearly visible mid-rib) are a number of shorter tentacles. These secrete protein-digesting enzymes which act on the insect's body, breaking it down to substances which can be absorbed by the plant. It is possible that bacterial action also is concerned in the breakdown of the insect prey. The whole process of trapping the insect and bringing it into the fold of the leaf takes about an hour and it will probably be two or three days before the leaf and its tentacles return to normal.

Although the round-leaved species is common on the peat moors, in the Catcott–Walton area and again around Westhay, the narrow-leaved species is becoming increasingly rare. In the early 1960s it grew fairly plentifully on part of Walton Heath, but it has not been found on that site since 1965.

BUTTERWORT (*Pinguicula vulgaris*) and PALE BUTTERWORT (*P. lusitanica*) are both fairly rare insectivorous plants and, to the delight of local botanists, Pale Butterwort reappeared in a field at Ashcott in 1967 after an absence of about ten years. Apart from this, it has been seen at several places in the Ashcott–Shapwick area, but never in any quantity. The leaves form a pale yellow rosette (though the 'pale' in its name applies to the pale purple flower) and like the Sundews, these leaves contain glands capable of secreting digestive enzymes and viscous fluids. There are no long hair-like tentacles, but the edges of the leaves roll inwards to increase their hold on the insects trapped on the sticky surface. Common Butterwort was noted from the peat moors before 1920 when it was recorded as very rare; there have been no records of it since then.

SPHAGNUM MOSS (*Sphagnum* spp) forms a blanket over some parts of the moor. It sucks up and retains water so that other plants can grow amongst it. Four species are particularly frequent and convert large areas into a typical 'carpet of flowers' during July and August. Bog Pimpernel (*Anagallis tenella*) has delicate pink flowers borne on stems only about 1in high. Forming an equally low-growing mat is the Ivy-leaved Bellflower (*Wahlenbergia hederacea*), which is much the smallest and most delicate of the bellflowers. The petals are a pale Cambridge blue and, mingling with the pink of the Pimpernel, produce an effect which one often strives in vain to emulate in a rockery. Milkwort (*Polygala vulgaris*) is slightly taller, the stems are usually about 3–4in high and its colour, though variable, is usually a deep blue. This provides a most delightful contrast to the delicacy of the pale pinks and pale blues. Marsh Pennywort (*Hydrocotyle vulgaris*) has rounded, deep green, glossy leaves like miniature water-lily leaves. Its name appears to over-value it since the leaves are rarely 1in across; Marsh Newpennywort would be a more appropriate title. The leaves seem just the right size, to the human eye, to combine with the Pimpernel, Bellflower and Milkwort; the leaf colour and texture is the perfect counterfoil to the delicacy of the other three plants. The flower of Marsh Pennywort itself is pale, yellow-green and unobtrusive. Near Catcott, another of these dwarf bog plants, Marsh St John's Wort (*Hypericum elodes*), adds a splash of

*The Lesser Butterfly Orchid (*Platanthera bifolia*) is one of the most delicate plants of the Peat Moors. The petals are ivory coloured and the flower has a very attractive scent.*

yellow to the flower carpet. Its leaves, covered in a down of fine hairs, appear a silver-greenish grey, while the flowers form the normal yellow star pattern of the family. One of Somerset's rarest plants, Marsh Pea (*Lathyrus palustris*) also grows in this region but its habitat is very limited and its continued presence on the moor is in some doubt.

Once a sphagnum bed has become established, its top layer is susceptible to rapid drying out, and drier acid micro habitats are set up. In these conditions, Heather (*Calluna vulgaris*), Bell Heather (*Erica cinerea*) and Cross-leaved Heath (*E. tetralix*) become common. Heathers and heaths are normally associated with dry sandy soils, but on the peat moors it is possible to find a heath plant growing within two or three inches of a sundew.

ORCHIDS of several species grow amongst these sphagnum beds. In the wetter parts can be found one of the rarest and certainly the most delicate, the Lesser Butterfly Orchid (*Platanthera bifolia*). The habitat of this lovely plant is very limited indeed. It occurs in a small area near Ashcott station and again near Walton. In a good year about fifty flowering spikes can be found but sometimes only one or two appear. The spike stands some 6–9in high and carries about six flowers. The flowers are a delicate ivory shade and the lip petal is divided so that the flower looks like a tied bow with the two trailing ends hanging downwards. In addition to its charming appearance, it is delightfully scented.

MARSH ORCHID (*Orchis praetermissa*) and HEATH ORCHID (*O. fuchsii*) also occur amongst the sphagnum, especially where it is a little drier. The Marsh Orchid is the taller of the two, often growing over 1ft high, and carries a spike of deep purple flowers marked with even deeper purple dots and lines. The spear-shaped leaves may also be marked with purple blotches. The Heath Orchids are very variable in their colour, ranging from white to deep pink, but with characteristic dark markings especially on the lip petal.

TWAYBLADE (*Listera ovata*) is common but not always noticed. When one has seen this orchid and 'got one's eye in', then it is comparatively easy to find. It grows on Shapwick Heath in the shade of trees and produces its green flowers in May. Its two oval leaves should be easy to recognise but are often obscured by low-lying vegetation.

Perhaps the least obvious of all the local orchids is the Frog Orchid (*Coeloglossum viride*), which has greenish petals and is usually only a few inches high. Although it normally grows on grassy hillsides, especially on calcareous soils, it does occur occasionally on the peat moor. Its appearance is very spasmodic and the last precise record was in 1963.

MILK PARSLEY (*Peucedanum palustre*), an uncommon member of the umbellifer family, is the plant eaten by caterpillars of the Swallowtail butterfly. This butterfly may once have been a native

*Bog Pimpernel (*Anagallis tenella*) used to form pink cushions set off against the green of the Sphagnum Moss. Unfortunately it is now becoming quite scarce on the Peat Moors.*

of these moors but, presumably owing to insufficient food, it is no longer present. Though generally uncommon, Milk Parsley is plentiful on parts of the peat moors and, if an attempt were made to reintroduce the butterfly, it is unlikely that it would fail through shortage of the food plant.

ROYAL FERN (*Osmunda regalis*), a rare inhabitant of the peat moors, is classified as one of the primitive ferns, since the spores are carried on non-photosynthesising structures. In most ferns the spores are to be found on the underside of the leaves, but Royal Fern produces a mass of very elegant yet sterile leaves. Carried up through the centre of the plant are the spore-bearing branches, like brown candelabra, emerging above the green foliage. The leaves are not as subdivided as in most species and therefore look less 'ferny'. This leaf shape, coupled with a more than usual upright habit and the large size which the clumps achieve, justifies the royal in its title.

Because of the acid soils, one of the first of the carr shrubs to become established on the peat moors is Bog Myrtle (*Myrica gale*). This shrub grows some 3–4ft high and its leaves are typically scented. So successful is this plant that in some areas around Ashcott a policy of deliberately cutting it back has been established. If this were not done, a patch particularly rich in sundew and other uncommon bog plants could easily become overgrown with Bog Myrtle and the more delicate ground flora would be driven out.

As on the rest of the Levels, alder and willows form much of the carr, but Birch (*Betula verrucosa*), Alder Buckthorn (*Frangula alnus*) and Hazel or Halse (*Corylus avellana*) are also fairly common on this acid soil. Where the bog surface has become a little drier, Gorse (or in Somersetshire—'Vuz') (*Ulex europaeus*) and then Pine (*Pinus sylvestris*) often follow on, but the more usual climactic trees are Beech (*Fagus sylvatica*) and Oak (*Quercus rober*). In some of the 'older' areas these trees have matured and typical woodland has formed, with an upper canopy layer; a shrub layer of such plants as honeysuckle and bramble; a herbaceous layer mostly of ferns and grasses, and a ground layer of mosses.

One unique feature of the peat moor is that the water table has, up to about 1970, remained more or less constant. On the peat beds the physical removal of the surface layers by the peat diggers has meant that the land level has dropped at about the same rate as the water level. Four features emphasise this factor. Firstly, the old Highbridge to Bournemouth railway track runs across the peat moors. Allowing for the metalling of the track, one can easily judge the level of the surface when the line was first laid in 1854. Although it was closed in 1966 and the track torn up and replaced by a roadway, one can still see how much the general level of the moor has dropped by comparison. Secondly, each of the old trees at the side of the line is growing out of an 'island' of raised peat. These 'islands' are some 4–6ft in height and indicate the drop in ground level since the trees started their life. Thirdly, but less reliable, are the droves or trackways. Like the railway line, these too are above the general moor level. Since peat is sometimes stacked on these droves while it dries, the levels here are liable to fluctuation. The fourth feature is that over much of the peat moors there are small pools of standing water. Even if the water cannot be seen it is only necessary to dig one's heels into the ground and the hollow thus formed will fill with brown peat-stained water.

The peat is not removed evenly over the whole area; it is cut from trenches and the higher ground left between the rows of trenches is used as a stacking area whilst the peat dries. In the earlier stages, the profile of the soil resembles battlements, but the peat is so soft that it squelches out sideways. The long-term result is that there is a general lowering of the ground level.

The grasses which occur on the moor are generally of poor grazing quality and so cattle are not very common; this means that much less of the land is held at the grass–meadow stage and can go on to the carr and woodland stages. Pine, beech and oak woods occur at various sites, and in a number of places one can see every stage in the succession from open water to climax woodland. These priseres, as they are called, are becoming increasingly rare and are valuable both scientifically and as part of our heritage.

Unfortunately, the trend at the moment is to extract more and more peat until the area becomes a lake. Conservationists are aware of the problem and it is hoped that something of this unique part of the world can be saved. This is discussed further in Chapter Ten.

*The Buttercup family have adapted so that they have members in almost every type of habitat. Spearwort (*Ranunculus flammula*) with its long narrow leaves is the Buttercup of the acidic peat soils.*

6

The Animal Life of the Levels (1)

The scientific names of the invertebrate animals are those used by Mellanby in *Animal life in Fresh Water* (1938). The names of the vertebrates are as in the *Penguin Dictionary of Natural History* (1966), except those of birds which are as used by Palmer & Balance in *Birds of Somerset* (1968).

A ditch like this, with a variety of plant life both on the banks and in the water, is very rich in invertebrate life.

Though the pattern of succession is dictated by the plants, a corresponding sequence can be seen in the animal life of the Levels. This pattern is not quite so clear cut, it is 'fuzzy round the edges'; partly because most animals have the power of movement so that one animal may utilise all, or nearly all, the stages in the surrounding plant succession, and partly because many animals undergo metamorphosis and may occupy different stages in the succession at different stages in their own life history.

Despite these considerations, a definite animal succession can be discerned.

When a ditch is cleaned out, animals as well as plants are killed in large numbers, but the more active animals can, in many cases, move away and then move back again into the open water when the disturbance is over. I have seen pond skaters on the water surface within a few hours of a ditch being cleaned out. On the other hand, pond snails cannot become really established again until there is sufficient vegetation for them. The speed with which many animals recolonise a patch of open water is therefore not so much a measure of their own speed of movement but of the rate at which the whole habitat develops.

Not only do animals need plants to give cover and as a supply of food, but a very complex pattern of feeding soon develops. At its simplest, this may be in the form of a chain; pondweeds are eaten by tadpoles; tadpoles are eaten by dragonfly larvae; dragonfly larvae are eaten by sticklebacks, and sticklebacks are eaten by perch; finally, the perch may be taken by a heron or a human. If these final carnivores (and humans are carnivores in this respect) remove too much food from the area, then the area can suffer. If food is thought of as a source of energy, then the energy removed from an area must be in proportion to the primary energy, ie sunlight, falling on it.

A simple food chain.

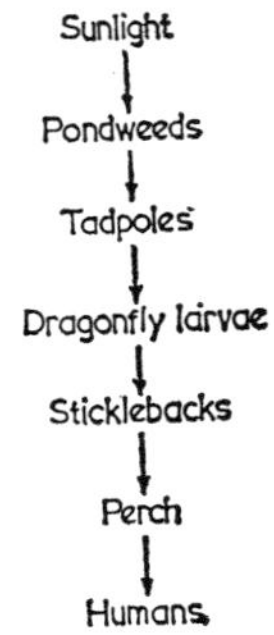

If the food, or energy, travelled in simple chains, these chains would be easy to unravel, and accurate and detailed conservation techniques could be developed.

Unfortunately, in the vast majority of cases, a much more complicated pattern, a food web, must be dealt with. In the example quoted above there are three major ways in which it is made complex. Firstly, the tadpoles are by no means the only animals to feed on the plants; thus a whole range of herbivores are involved. Similarly, large numbers of animals feed on tadpoles and these too have to be considered. Secondly, the tadpoles become carnivorous as they grow older, and feed on a variety of small animals. Thirdly, a large dragonfly larva may take a small stickleback, but a large stickleback may take a small dragonfly larva.

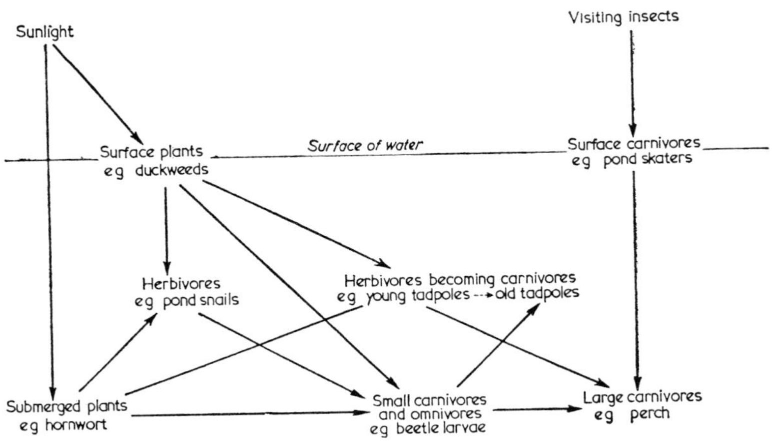

Simplified version of a food web as it occurs in a ditch.

If this is extended to cover the whole of life in a ditch, it is necessary to include such animals as moths, which live outside the habitat but occasionally land on the water surface and are fed on by surface feeders, such as pond skaters. These in turn play their part in the food web.

General work on animal populations shows that most of them

steadily rise to a peak and then drop sharply before starting another rise. A simple herbivore, such as the water snail, in a ditch with an ample food supply will grow and reproduce freely. This state of affairs will continue for a while but eventually two 'controls' will apply. Firstly, as the animal population rises so the amount of food available for each individual will decline. This does not necessarily mean that they will starve to death but rather that they will be less healthy and more prone to disease and parasite attack. Secondly, the predators of the water snail will move into that ditch. These may be leeches which swim into the water-snail colony or water birds which can reach it overland. The predator population, with a plentiful supply of snails, will now rise. This in turn puts more pressure on the snails and so their population will drop. As this happens, so the predators put even more pressure on the remaining snails, whose population will drop drastically.

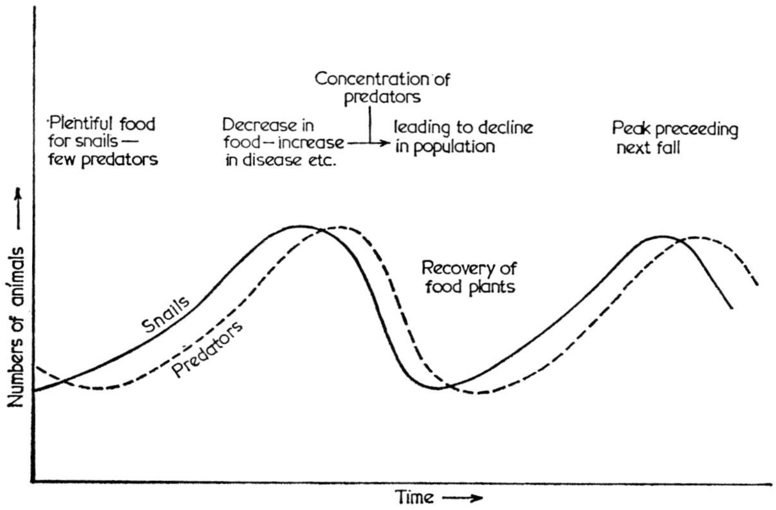

Graph to illustrate the rise and fall in predator-prey populations.

The predator population in turn will drop and they will either produce fewer young or move into another area. With the drop in the snail population the primary food plants will regenerate and once again the snails will start to build up.

Other work has revealed the food substances of the various organisms and, especially in the last ten years, ecologists have been trying to estimate the 'energy values' of the various foods. This has led to the concept of measuring the energy flow through the system.

Thus, in a variety of ways this very complex natural pattern is beginning to be unravelled and understood. The main point which does emerge clearly is that the whole of the life of the area is so closely interwoven that an alteration of one factor 'echoes' throughout the system. So, changes in the drainage pattern will not only affect the plant life but be reflected in the dependent animal population.

While it is possible to make reasonably reliable counts of plants in an area, it is considerably more difficult to do so in the case of animals. A table of 'common-ness' among animals would contain so much guess work that it would be almost worthless. One must also take into account the fact that one large predator feeds on, and therefore 'equals', a number of smaller animals, which in turn 'equal' a much greater number of even smaller organisms. For these reasons, I have separated the animals in two groups: the invertebrates and the vertebrates. Within each group, the animals are arranged in 'succession' order rather than in order of population size.

The invertebrates of the ditches

When a ditch is cleaned out, the habitat consists of an area of open water with very little vegetation. At this stage the main food supply is either the organic material contained in the mud at the bottom or animals, such as insects, which fall on to the surface and become trapped. The early life in a ditch therefore consists usually of microscopic or semi microscopic mud feeders and the larger surface feeders.

Surface feeders

POND SKATERS (*Gerris* spp) are one of the earliest visible invaders of a ditch. Two of the ten species occurring in Britain, *G. lacustris* (L) and *G. odontogaster* (Zett), have definitely been identified from Sedgemoor and three more probably occur. They are long narrow insects (about 1·5cm long), with the second and third pairs of legs particularly elongated. These, in conjunction with their terminal pads, support the weight of the insect on the surface film of the water. Normally the insect glides over the surface with a typical skating movement, but it can jump from the surface and, if it has fully developed wings, it can fly. Pond skaters belong to the group of insects generally called bugs because of their piercing and sucking mouths. Their method of feeding is to 'skate' over to an insect which is trapped on the water surface. They use their front legs to hold their prey, then stab it with a hollow, hypodermic-needle-like mouth called a rostrum and probably pump digestive enzymes into it. The skater then sucks back the liquid part of the prey.

The eggs are laid in batches and usually stuck to plants just below the water surface. They hatch into a larval form and the adults emerge after what is probably the fifth larval stage about July–August. Like all surface dwellers, they must face the problem of the water icing over during the winter and evidence points to hibernation on land as their method of survival.

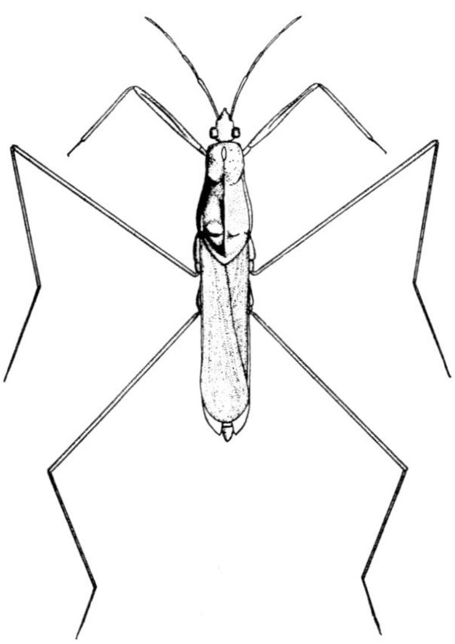

*Pond skater (*Gerris lacustris*).*

THE WATER MEASURER (*Hydrometra stagnorum*) is less common

than the pond skater of the *Gerris* species, and whereas the skater is normally found in groups, the Water Measurer is usually seen alone. It looks like a small thin pond skater, but has an exceptionally long thin head. It also differs in its feeding methods. The Water Measurer's prey is the collection of small insects and crustaceans, which live below the water surface but must come to the surface to take in air. This feeding has been described by Watson as follows: 'While standing on the water it can feel the small pulsations set up by a water-flea swimming just under the water film, whereupon it dips its long slender rostrum into the water, feeling around with the flexible tip, and shifting its position until the little crustacean comes near. Then with a sudden, tiny, quick jerk it harpoons the unfortunate flea with its strongly barbed stylets. If the water-flea is small it is pulled through the surface film and carried about on the end of the rostrum. A large water-flea will put up a fight, but the *hydrometra* plays it like a fisherman, using its rostrum as a rod and the stylets as a line, until some vital organ is damaged.'

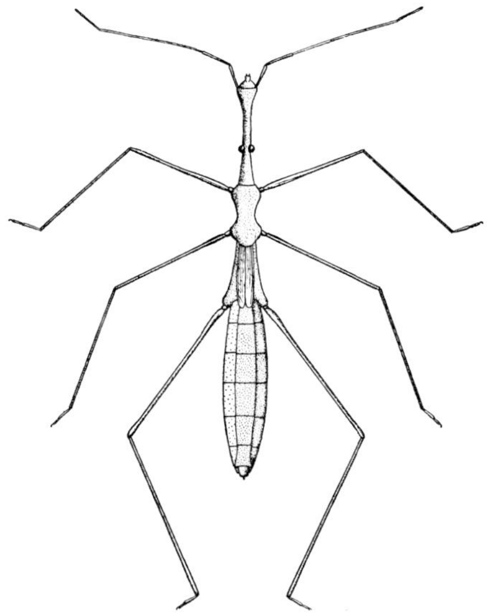

*Water Measurer (*Hydrometra stagnorum*).*

WATER CRICKETS (*Velia currens* and *Microvelia reticulata*) are shorter and fatter than pond skaters. Although usually found near the bank where the current is reduced, they can move easily over the water surface. Like *Gerris*, they feed on insects and other animals trapped on the surface and washed along to them. There is some doubt as to whether the British representative of a third genus of Water Cricket (*Mesovelia furcata*) is to be found on Sedgemoor or not.

Mud dwellers

FLATWORMS (*Turbellarians* such as *Planaria* spp) are typical mud dwellers. Most of them are about 1cm long and either black or dark brown. Their bodies are flattened dorsiventrally and they appear to glide over the surface of the substrate. They are propelled by the movement of minute hair-like cilia which cover their bodies. Occasionally the internal muscles are used and the animal swims, rather badly, with a 'sea-serpent' type of movement. The mouth is on the underside and in many species the pharynx can be everted so that the feeding action looks rather as if the animal is 'vacuum-cleaning' the mud surface. Flatworms are carnivorous, their food ranging from microscopic forms to young fish. The species which attack relatively large prey, such as fish, wrap themselves round their food and pour digestive juices on to it before engulfing it. If a flatworm is put into a dish of water its movements are extremely irregular, but if a stone is also placed in the dish, these irregular movements will eventually bring the animal under the stone; once there, it becomes quiescent. During the daytime, most planarians keep out of strong light by taking cover under dead vegetation or in the small irregularities found in the ditch bank; at night they emerge and feed.

All animals, aquatic or otherwise, must take in oxygen. The higher animals have evolved many ways of doing this, even though they live below the water surface, but the simple forms are able to absorb oxygen from the surrounding water through the whole of their body surface. The waste carbon-dioxide is expelled in the same way. As animals increase in size, the ratio of surface area to volume decreases. It is, therefore, only the small animals which can carry out their gaseous exchange by simple diffusion through the body wall. Planarians are helped in this respect in that the extreme flattening of the body increases the surface area.

TRUE WORMS (*Annelida*) are best known through their terrestrial representatives, such as earthworms. However, large numbers of this group are either freshwater aquatic or marine, and they exhibit quite a variety of form and shape within the general framework of a segmented body. The Square-tailed Worm (*Eiseniella tetrahedra*) is very similar to a small common earthworm and feeds on organic material in the mud in the same way as the earthworm feeds in the soil. *Chaetogaster* (it has no common name) is much smaller, about ½in long, but transparent. This worm is often found inside occupied snail shells. This is a curious parallel with the marine worm, which is often found sharing a shell with a hermit crab. The third worm to be identified from Sedgemoor is *Stylaria*. It is also transparent but distinguished by a long thin proboscis and rows of very long bristles along its body. In this species the bristles have retained what was probably their original function, they are used for swimming. All three species obtain their oxygen through blood vessels close to the body surface; they breathe through their skin.

SWAN MUSSELS (*Anodonta cygnea*) and PEA-SHELL COCKLES (*Neritina fluviatilis* and *Pisidium* spp) are widespread yet rarely seen alive. These bivalve molluscs each have a large foot which is used to drag the whole animal into the mud where it lies almost buried. The foot is protruded between the two shells and pushed down into the mud. The tip then swells so that it acts as an anchor and, by contracting along its length, the foot pulls the rest of the body downwards. Eventually, the openings of two tubes are all that remain visible. Water is drawn into one of these tubes and, as it passes through the body of the animal, oxygen and minute food particles are extracted. The water is then passed out through the second tube, usually setting up small disturbances in the mud which can give away the position of the animal. It is presumably these signs which are recognised by one of its chief predators, the heron. The dry shells of Swan Mussels are a common sight along the banks of the larger rhynes and drains, sometimes there is a shell every few paces. Small shells, less than 3in, are quite uncommon and one can only assume that in some way the heron can recognise the larger specimens. The method by which young mussels are dispersed is most unusual; the larvae are parasitic and

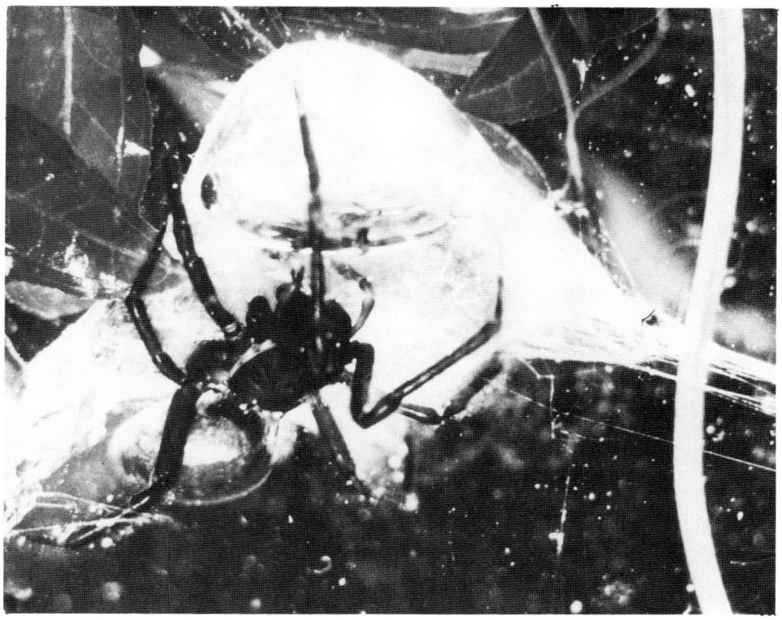

The Water Spider spins a web under water. It then makes repeated visits to get air from the surface until the web forms an air bell in which it can live.

attach themselves to the gills or skins of fish. They feed on the tissue of the fish until they eventually drop off and become free living.

As the amount of vegetation in a ditch increases, so, up to a point, the populations and varieties of animals also increase; and the food web becomes more complex. It is extremely difficult to estimate the populations of various species of animals, but from my own observations it would appear that a ditch with a well-established group of plants in the water and showing only the beginnings of 'encroachment' from the sides gives the richest yields of animals. These range from microscopic protozoans up to large vertebrates, such as fish and an occasional otter, and include the medium-sized insects and other invertebrates which are the easiest to find and observe. Since these show a variety of adaptations to life in water and form the central part of the food web, they are a particularly rewarding group of animals to study.

Animals from the middle of the ditches

POND SNAILS (*Gastropoda*) occur in enormous numbers in all the waterways. As vegetarians they form an early link in the food web, acting as intermediaries between the primary producers, the plants, and the host of carnivores. Like land snails, they feed by a radula, a rasp-like band of small teeth which tears away at the plant food. Whether they get the calcium needed for their shell from the plants or from the salts in the water is not clear, but certainly the pond snail population on the acid peat moors is considerably smaller than elsewhere on Sedgemoor. Sixteen species have so far been identified with the Common Pond-snail (*Limnaea stagnalis*) as the largest (up to 2in) and the Wandering Pond-snail (*L.*

pereger) as the commonest. In May it is difficult to pull out a handful of weed without finding its egg masses. These transparent masses are about 1in long and 7–8mm wide, and contain something like forty eggs which hatch, without a larval stage, into young snails. Apart from forming a food supply for the carnivores, one species, the Dwarfed Snail (*L. truncatula*) acts as an intermediate host for the Sheep Liver Fluke. Since this snail is to be found on land as well as in the water, it can easily carry the infection. Amongst the water snails are six species of Ram's Horn (*Planorbis*). These have a very distinctive flat spiral shell and are probably better adapted physiologically to survive in stagnant water. Instead of the blue-green haemocyanin pigment which occurs in most snails, this genus has red haemoglobin as an oxygen carrier in its blood. Occasionally albino forms can be found and in these the red blood shows through, making them popular for aquaria.

Although most of this genus occasionally come to the surface to take in air, they are essentially bottom feeders living on the detritus which sinks down.

WATER LICE (*Asellus* spp), sometimes called Hog-lice or Water Slaters, are also common feeders on detritus. In general they appear very much like Wood-lice, but lack their ability to roll up when threatened. With two pairs of antennae, four pairs of mouth parts, eight pairs of legs and five broad gills, they seem particularly vulnerable when one remembers that they can be attacked from below. Yet, in an aquarium, sticklebacks will often ignore them and choose prey which seems more difficult to catch. However, aquarium work also shows that given ideal conditions, these water lice breed very rapidly. Since the numbers in a ditch remain more or less constant, one can only conclude that, like the snails, they form an important link between the plants and the hunting animals.

FRESHWATER SHRIMPS (*Gammarus* spp) are less common than water lice on Sedgemoor. In fact, the proportions of the two groups gives a good guide to the amount of oxygen in the water; *Gammarus* lives where there is a high oxygen content and *Asellus* where it is low. The two genera are easy to distinguish since *Asellus* is flattened dorsiventrally and a brownish colour, while *Gammarus* is laterally flattened and usually a slate-grey colour. Although both feed on decaying organic matter, the so-called shrimp is usually found in association with fresh green plant life; presumably the oxygen given off in photosynthesis is the factor which influences this distribution.

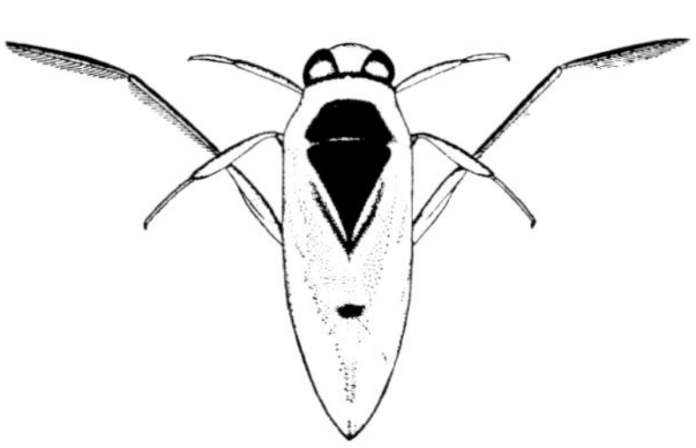

*Water Boatman (*Notonecta*).*

WATER BOATMEN (*Notonecta* and *Corixa* spp) belong to the family of Water-bugs and are one of the commonest and most easily observed groups of predators. The larger species are about $\frac{1}{2}$in long, with an oval body. The long, third pair of legs has a number of stiff hairs along its distal segments; and the limb has a striking

Newly hatched Raft Spiders.

The Raft Spider, Britain's largest spider, hunts on the surface of the water.

resemblance to an oar in both shape and function. Two species of *Notonecta* have been identified from Sedgemoor, both characterised by the very long hind legs and the habit of swimming upside down. There are four rows of hairs on the ventral surface, which form two channels. When the insect is at the surface, these channels fill with air; this alters the centre of gravity, so that the Boatman swims with the ventral surface uppermost. It also means that the insect is lighter than water and rests just below the water surface. From here it will take any prey which lands on the surface, but it is a powerful swimmer and preys on a variety of animals, such as tadpoles, small fish and other insects. It tackles large prey with its beak-like mouth with which it pierces and then sucks the juices from its food source. Since it can easily and painfully penetrate human skin, it should be handled with care.

Of the thirty-six species of *Corixidae,* ten are certainly found on Sedgemoor and another seven are probably present. Sometimes called the Lesser Water Boatmen, these insects are generally smaller and heavier than the *Notonectidae,* and swim 'the right way up'. They also differ in that the third pair of legs is not so pronounced; often it is no longer than the second pair. A further difference is that they normally feed by sucking up micro-organisms and detritus from the bottom and only come to the surface to take in air.

In the adult stage, all the members of this group can fly and therefore quickly colonise a suitable habitat. Most survive the winter as adults and lay their eggs on aquatic plants in spring. By mid-summer they are so common that it is exceptional if they are not found with every sweep of a pond net.

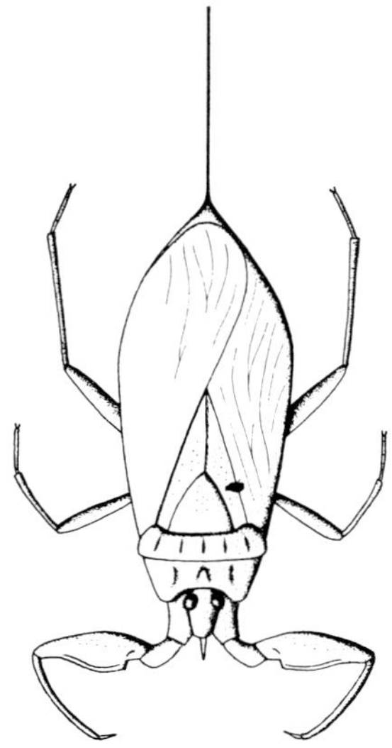

*Water Scorpion (*Nepa cinerea*)*

The WATER SCORPION (*Nepa cinerea*), another Water-bug, is a fascinating creature. At first glance, an adult resembles a brown decaying willow leaf, about 1½in long. This, coupled with its habit of remaining close to the bank, makes it difficult to find. On close examination one can see its unusual first pair of legs, which are wider than the others and held in a typical 'scorpion' manner. These grasp an animal when it comes within reach, each leg closing rather like a penknife snapping shut. This holds the prey up to the piercing mouthpart, which impales it and then sucks it out. Normally the Water Scorpion hunts among the plants near the edge of the ditch and just below the surface. To get its oxygen it has evolved a breathing tube at its hind end. The tip of this tube protrudes above the surface, keeping the insect in contact with the air while it awaits its prey.

The WATER STICK INSECT (*Ranatra linearis*) is truly British in that it might have been designed by a series of compromises. It is a bug which looks like a scorpion imitating a stick insect. Its general body plan is similar to that of the Water Scorpion, but the animal is much more slender and only about half the length. It is perhaps more venturesome in moving away from the bank than its relative, but its feeding habits are almost the same.

WHIRLIGIG BEETLES (*Gyrinidae*), like the Water Boatmen, are so common that one takes them for granted. These are the small beetles which swim very quickly in circles on the surface of the water. Their middle and hind legs have long folding swimming hairs, their bodies are beautifully streamlined and their eyes so divided that the upper part can see above the surface while the lower section can see below. Being surface living, they normally have no problem about obtaining oxygen; but when they dive, which they do readily on the approach of danger, they carry an air bubble down with them. The larvae, which can be found in mid-summer, are omnivorous; but the adults are mostly insectivorous and it seems likely that their surface movements are in

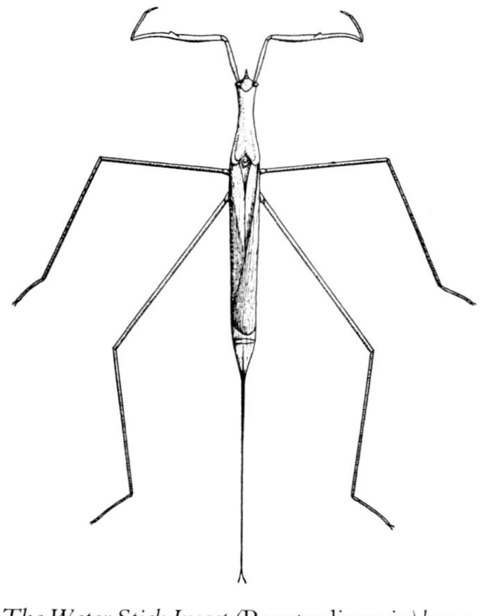

*The Water Stick Insect (*Ranatra linearis*) has a 'praying mantis' appearance as it stalks and captures its prey.*

The Water Stick insect

some way connected with feeding. Five species have been identified from the Sedgemoor area.

WATER DIVING BEETLES (*Dytiscidae*) are represented by fifty-nine species identified from Sedgemoor. Of these, the best known is the Great Diving-beetle (*Dytiscus marginalis*), which reaches a length of about 1in, but many members of the family are much smaller. The adults are good swimmers, their hind legs being flattened and covered with swimming hairs. The air supply is obtained at the surface and taken down as a bubble between the elytra and the abdomen. The *Dytiscids* are voracious carnivores and will attack almost any animal of their own size; the larvae are especially ferocious, their mouth-parts mainly consisting of a pair of prominent hollow fangs, which act like hypodermic needles; digestive enzymes are pumped into the victim and the dissolved food then sucked back. This habit is similar to the feeding methods of water bugs.

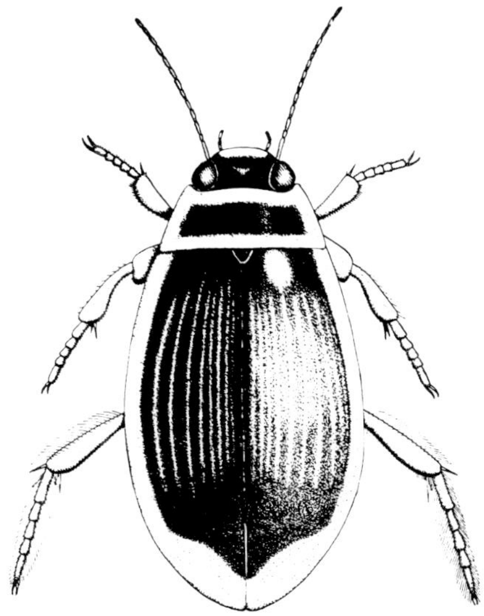

*Water Diving Beetle (*Dytiscus marginalis*).*

At first glance, the GREAT SILVER WATER BEETLE (*Hydrophilus piceus*) looks like a *Dytiscid*, but its life history and habits are quite different. It is our largest beetle (the Stag Beetle is longer, but its body smaller); though most of the other members of this family—twenty-three of which occur on Sedgemoor—are less than 1cm long. As a group, they are poor swimmers, moving each leg separately rather than 'pulling together'. This is no great handicap, as they are vegetarian, although the larvae are carnivorous. The Great Silver Water Beetle larva is rather like a long (7cm) black caterpillar; its chief food is pond snails. Although it is aquatic, I have seen this beetle crawling over a surface film of duckweed to find its prey.

*The Musk Beetle (*Aromia moschata*) has a larval form whose favourite food is the living wood of trees such as Willow and Alder.*

*The adult of the Great Silver Beetle (*Hydrophilus piceus*) grows to about 4 cms and the larva to about 6 cms.*

LEECHES (*Hirudinea*) are extremely common. The easiest way of catching them is to pull out a handful of green algae. Within a few minutes they can be seen wriggling up to the surface of the mass. The commonest species is *Herpobdella octoculata*, but three other species, including the Horse Leech (*Haemopsis sanguisuga*) and the Medicinal Leech (*Hirudo medicinalis*), have been identified at various times. Although related to earthworms, leeches move in characteristic ways of their own. Their normal method is to use the suckers at each end of their body and move in a series of loops, but occasionally they leave the supporting vegetation and swim by undulating their bodies in the way usually ascribed to sea serpents. When feeding, leeches will attack most soft-bodied creatures, pond snails being particularly vulnerable.

CADDIS FLIES (*Trichoptera*) are brownish moth-like insects in the adult stage, but locally their larvae are aquatic. When they hatch in summer, the larvae usually make a portable protective case, consisting of a silken web forming an inner tube and a mass of foreign material cemented on to the outside. Other species, living in fast-flowing water, may be free living and web spinning, or they may use small pebbles and grit as an outer case layer. The Sedgemoor species use mainly vegetation, either fresh or rotting, or fine silt grains to form this outer coat. The group which makes up most of the twenty-nine species identified from the Levels contains both active carnivores and more sluggish herbivores. They live in their cases with the head and thorax protruding so that their legs are free and they can crawl, rather clumsily, through the vegetation. The abdomen is grub-like, except that it carries external gills and, on the last segment, a pair of hooks with which it holds the case. When pupating, the normal practice is to withdraw into the case and seal the anterior end. When the internal changes have been completed, the insect bites its way out of the case, swims to the surface and, after drying its wings, takes to the air.

MOSQUITOES, like Caddis Flies, have aquatic pre-adult stages. The smallest member of the family, the Common Gnat (*Culex pipiens*), occurs everywhere and is relatively harmless. The larger, dark-spotted species *Theobaldia annulata*, a blood-sucking form which often raises irritant swellings, and the Horsefly or Cleg (*Haematopota pluvialis*), another blood-sucking insect, frequently occur on Shapwick Heath, so it is advisable to wear an insect repellent when visiting the area on a summer evening. It is the female mosquito which sucks blood, it seems that she requires the extra protein before being able to lay her eggs; otherwise both sexes feed on plant juices. The eggs are laid on water, either supported by their own air floats or in batches so that they float like a raft. The larvae which hatch out normally hang in the water, supported under the surface tension film. Their air supply is obtained by a small tube, a siphon, which breaks through the surface film; a similar device is used in the pupal stage. As usual, the larval stage is the feeding one. Each larva is equipped with a pair of mouth brushes, which move so that a current of water, carrying microscopic food, is swept towards the mouth. In the pupal stage, the insect looks like a 'comma' suspended in the water by its breathing-tubes. As the adults hatch out, the empty pupal case provides a small floating buoy on which to stand while they expand and dry their wings before flying off.

DRAGONFLIES and DAMSELFLIES (*Odonata*) are probably the most dramatic of the invertebrate forms. As larvae they are voracious hunters, and as adults they make superb fliers and are extremely attractive. The yellow and black markings on the body of the Southern Aeshna (*Aeshna cyanea*) and the blue and yellow Broad-bodied Libellula (*Libellula depressa*), hovering and then darting away over the alder carr, seem to typify a Sedgemoor summer's day. Altogether, twenty-five species have been identified with certainty and three others may occur. Of the species present, the blue and the red Damselflies are by far the commonest. Not only are the adults relatively slender, the larvae of the Damselfly are thin and delicate when compared to those of the heavier Dragonfly. They have three tail appendages; the Damselfly's look like three wings and the Dragonfly's are usually very short indeed. These tail appendages are, as in a number of other animals, associated with breathing, and sometimes called gills. The unique feature of this group is the so-called face mask. They are carnivorous; their

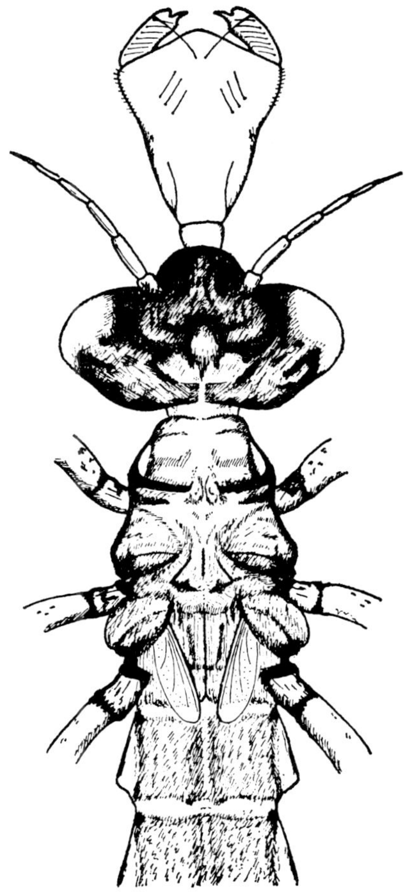

Head of Dragonfly larva, with the mask in the forward position.

*A Broad-bodied Dragonfly (*Libellula depressa*) resting on Cotton Grass.*

feeding method involves ambushing or stalking their prey, which can be almost any form of animal life. When the food is within reach, the lower lip is shot forward. In profile it is shaped rather like a letter Z, the upper horizontal line being attached to the rest of the head and the two lower lines being hinged and able to extend forward and to the right. The prey is then held in the jaws and pulled back to the other mouth parts. It is the adult Dragonfly which normally attracts our attention. Recognisable Dragonflies have been found amongst our earliest fossils; it would seem that the evolutionary process has been unable to improve on them in all that time.

Invertebrates of the meadows

Taking the whole of Sedgemoor into consideration—the ditches, the pastures and the villages—the variety of insect life is staggering. Despite the fact that no entomologist has yet concentrated on the Somerset Levels and these records are made almost in passing, 599 species of moth, 41 species of butterfly and 531 species of beetle have been definitely identified from the moors. Insects located on the fringes of the area have been classed as belonging to the Levels if their food plant or prey is commonly found there and not on the surrounding hills; all those cases where the food is so widespread that the origin of the insect is in doubt have been excluded from the above figures.

Lack of information makes it difficult to assess the relative importance of the various species. Because of their size and frequency, Meadow Brown butterflies (*Maniola jurtina*) appear to dominate the scene in July. They are particularly attracted to purple flowers, and thistles and hard-heads often have several butterflies on the same flowerhead. Since the larvae feed on grasses, there is no shortage of food for them.

At the other end of the frequency scale is the Swallowtail butterfly (*Papilio machaon*), a species which is both handsome and rare. The main food of the larvae is Milk Parsley, which grows

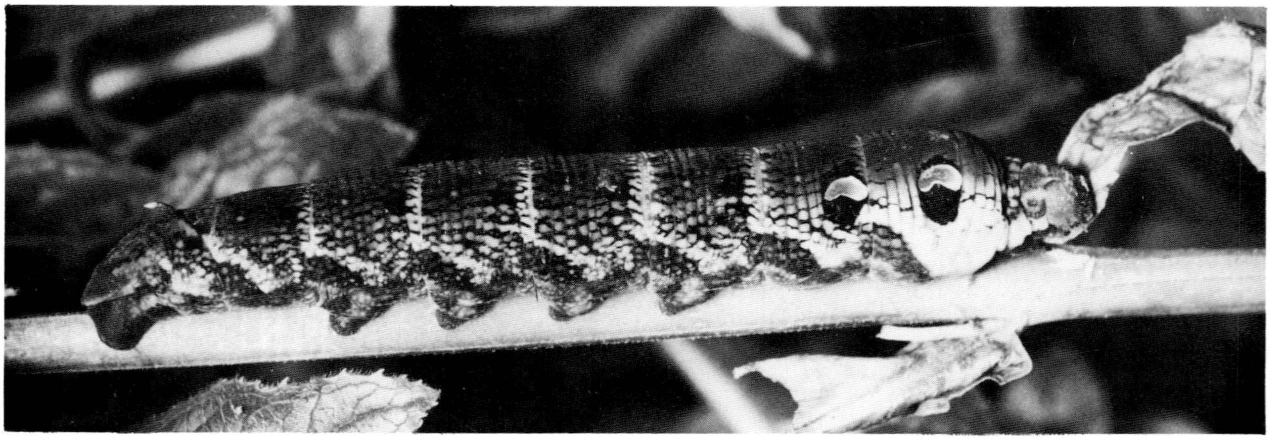

*The caterpillar of the Elephant Hawk-moth (*Deilephila elpenor*) is often found feeding on water-side plants.*

quite well on Shapwick Heath. It seems likely therefore that the handful of specimens recorded in the last century were local ones and neither migrants nor strays. The distribution of Milk Parsley in that period is not known, but was probably more widespread than it is today. However, this does not explain the butterfly's disappearance nor why attempts to re-establish it failed. In 1932, both eggs and pupae were put out on the moor. The pupae were protected in breeding cages and eventually forty adults emerged in good condition. In June of that year, a supply of eggs were attached to their food plants as an additional method of building up the population. Unfortunately these attempts at re-colonisation were unsuccessful and this gorgeous butterfly must be considered extinct on Sedgemoor.

An insect which seems to be increasing, at least on Shapwick Heath, is the Glow-worm (*Lampyris noctiluca*). The light is given off by the female to attract the male. It is not unusual to see half a dozen of these cold blue lights on a late summer evening on the Heath.

Perhaps because it is so closely tied up with the plant succession, my own special delight is to find the White Admiral butterfly (*Limenitis camilla*). Its name is possibly a corruption of White Admirable; both the adult butterfly with its white-marked purple-brown wings and the pupa with metallic colours of gold-green and purple have a very handsome appearance. Technically, it is a secondary woodland species. The larvae feed on honeysuckle; to support this butterfly, the succession must have advanced not only to woodland, but to the secondary features of climbing plants. On Sedgemoor, most of the records come from either Shapwick Heath or Walton Heath, where the plant sequence is sufficiently far advanced into woodland to form a suitable habitat for this admirable butterfly.

*The Emperor Moth (*Saturnia pavonia*) is striking in its adult stage. The larvae feed on a range of marsh plants. Sallow is particularly chosen.*

*The caterpillar of the Drinker Moth (*Philudoria potatoria*) feeds on grasses and since it gets its name from its habit of drinking dew, the damp grasses of the Levels are ideal food plants.*

7
The Animal Life of the Levels (2)

Vertebrate life excluding birds

All five classes of vertebrates: fish, amphibia, reptiles, birds and mammals are well represented on Sedgemoor. An overall picture of their past history can be deduced from what is known of the presence of various animals and the type of habitat that existed, but without reliable records it is difficult to estimate the numbers of species.

In general, the larger mammalian carnivores and omnivores, the wolves and the wild boars which existed during the period of the lake villages, were the final links in the food chains. Once they had reached maturity they were relatively free from other predators, except man, and their death would mostly have occurred as a result of disease. It is unlikely that their bodies were left to rot. Scavengers, ranging from maggots to crows, would have fed on them; those which died in water would have been similarly preyed upon by a range of aquatic animals, from micro organisms to eels.

Until humans populated Sedgemoor in large numbers, it was a very self-contained area. The energy required by the whole living complex came from the sun and from then on it was cycled and re-cycled through the system. Even the early human settlers were part of this system and virtually nothing was imported into or exported from the area. It fed and housed itself.

This pattern continued with only very slight changes up to the end of the eighteenth century. From then onwards, man has turned Sedgemoor into a producing area. The sun's energy is still used by plants, but these are chiefly of use to man, either to feed him or his animals.

The one animal, apart from man, which now dominates is the cow, and the main pattern today is a simple one. The sun's energy is absorbed by the grass, which in turn goes to produce beef, cheese and so on. This is managed successfully and the area produces more energy in the way of these foods than its own population requires. As a result, Sedgemoor is now an exporting area, sending its dairy products to the world outside.

The old wild moor where animals lived, ate, fought and died in their own marshy world has given way to a man-controlled

system. The waterways were put into order to drain the moors; then the animals were put into order to give as large a yield as possible. In establishing this system, most of the larger animals which might have interfered with it have been eliminated. We know that wild boar, elk, red deer, roe deer, wild cat, beaver, marten and polecat were all present in the original pattern; it is also very probable that wolves and bears were too. None of these now lives on Sedgemoor. Because of their numbers, small mammals such as voles and mice have survived, and, as in the rest of Britain, they have been joined by rabbits and rats.

Just as the ditches provided an alternative habitat for aquatic plants, so they provided a new place for fish, amphibia and grass snakes. Because fish provide us with a leisure activity (their contribution to our food supply is very small indeed) more have been introduced, and it is possible that the fish population is as high as it ever was.

The mud flats at the mouth of the River Parrett give us some idea of what the Levels might have looked like about 5000 years ago.

Few people can identify species of frog, toad, newt, snake and lizard; consequently, the records of amphibia and reptiles in the area are very scanty. They are reasonably plentiful, but there is no evidence to show how their population has changed.

On the other hand, birds have been well recorded and because they have successfully adapted to a very wide variety of habitats they convey a good idea of the pattern of change. For this reason I have given the birds a section of their own, see Chapter Eight.

I have not attempted to describe or even list all the various species of vertebrates, but have selected those which either illustrate the general trend or show some feature of special interest.

The fish

The earliest definite record of fish comes from the lake villages. Roach (*Rutilus rutilus*), Trout (*Salmo trutta*), Shad (*Clupea* spp), Perch (*Perca fluviatilis*) and Pike (*Esox lucius*) have all been identified. A fourteenth-century banquet menu shows that Salmon (*Salmo salar*), Bream (*Abramis brama*), Minnows (*Phoxinus phoxinus*) and Eels (*Anguilla anguilla*) were also present. The Roach, which prefers deepish weedy water, would have found these conditions in the rivers, the cut-off ox-bows and the larger pools. Feeding on small crustaceae and worms, the Bream occupies a similar habitat. These two can be considered typical Sedgemoor fish.

Salmon and Trout are fish of clear running streams and still occur to some extent in the rivers. The river authorities have made attempts to restock them, but the general pattern is one of a declining population. The upper reaches of the River Tone and the River Brue are now the only original places where the Brown Trout can be found in any numbers. With the introduction of Rainbow Trout into the reservoirs, these have superceded the rivers as areas where Trout are fished for sport. Salmon were fished for from Bridgwater until a few years ago. The normal practice was to net them on their migratory swims, but the numbers are so few that this no longer happens. Most small boys will talk about 'minnows', but invariably the fish they refer to are Sticklebacks. Like Trout, Minnows are restricted to the upper reaches of the rivers and rarely appear on Sedgemoor proper.

It is not easy to explain the decline in population of these fish. Overfishing may be part of the answer, and also pollution. The water in the tidal reaches of the rivers looks filthy, but this is largely due to the inorganic muds and silts which are brought down and then washed backwards and forwards with the tides. Because it makes the water opaque and because of the changing salinity and changing water levels, no appreciable plant life establishes itself in the river or on the banks which are uncovered at low tide. This absence of plant life means that both oxygen and food are scarce, but these are not new conditions—the lower

rivers have always been much the same. If the water is becoming polluted, it is far more likely to be due to a general increase in the organic matter entering the river. This organic material provides food for bacteria and, in turn, the bacteria extract oxygen from the water. When the oxygen content is already low, a relatively slight increase in bacterial activity can swing the balance so that Salmon and Trout can no longer tolerate the new conditions. Even this explanation does not give a complete answer; in 1851 Salmon were recorded as 'not so common as formerly'.

Fish traps, often made from local withies at the mouth of the River Parrett.

Perch and Pike occur in all the larger waterways, West Sedgemoor Main Drain and King's Sedgemoor Drain carrying particularly large numbers. Perch are often to be seen in large feeding shoals inhabiting the slow-moving clear sections of the drains and rivers. Both Perch and Pike must be able to see their prey and consequently avoid opaque muddy water. Pike of up to 18lb have been taken, but for most of the waterways a 10lb fish is considered large. Pike are one of the few fish which really stalk their prey. Most fish use their caudal (tail) fin for forward movement, but when a Pike has sighted its prey it moves forward by sending ripples along its dorsal fin. This movement is hidden by the hump of the back and consequently there is no fin movement visible which could alert the prey. Once the Pike is within striking distance, it uses its powerful body muscles and caudal fin to make the final dash to seize its food.

As might be expected from the state of the drains and rivers, bottom-feeding fish are quite common. Tench thrives in the muddier reaches and especially where aquatic plant life is rich; it must have succeeded very well in the pre-drainage days. Large fish living in shallow water have to face the problem of it icing over in winter. Surface ice does not necessarily kill the fish, but it does reduce the amount of available oxygen and cuts the fish off from surface food. Tench feeds on the small crustaceae and molluscs living on the mud or amongst the water plants; it is not dependent on food at the surface of the water. During winter it becomes torpid, a form of hibernation, and buries itself in the mud. In this way, it is protected from the ice and, at the same time, its oxygen intake is at a minimum.

In spring vast numbers of elvers enter the Severn Estuary and ascend the rivers. These start their life as eggs in the Sargasso Sea and the larvae migrate across the Atlantic. During this stage of their life history they are almost transparent, willow-leaf-shaped larvae, called *Leptocephalus*. The movement across the Atlantic takes about three years; in their final winter at sea, they change into the recognisable eel or elver shape. They are now about 3in long and about a thousand of them weigh 1lb; it is in this form that they move into the fresh water. Where there are obstructions, such as the old lock gates on the Bridgwater–Taunton Canal, they are so thick in the water that they can be scooped out by the bucketful. There are still a few people who catch them at this stage to make elver pie, a local dish. A drop in the Baltic eel population has led to a small industry growing up in the last few years: local elvers are trapped, flown to the Baltic and released there. These eels are then re-caught, for food, when they make their final migration back to the sea.

On Sedgemoor, the elvers which survive the movement up river move out into all the smaller ditches, rhynes and ponds. By travelling usually at night through wet grass, they can move overland and so reach ponds which are landlocked. Here they feed on worms and a host of aquatic forms; the males attaining a length of about 2ft and living about fourteen years, and the females growing up to about 5ft and reaching an age of forty years. These larger eels have been known to take frogs, water birds and water voles. They are known as yellow eels due to the colouring of their undersides, but towards the end of their life they turn silver. It is then that they start their journey back to the Sargasso Sea where they become sexually mature, mate and die.

One very unusual group of fish found in the rivers are the Lampreys. Occasional large specimens (up to 3ft) of the Sea Lamprey (*Petromyzon marinus*) have been taken from the River Parrett, and the smaller River Lamprey (*Lampetra fluviatilis*) has been recorded from the fresh water stretches of several of the rivers.

Unlike all other fish, the Lampreys (and the Hagfish) have not only retained a cartilaginous skeleton, but have followed an evolutionary line which has excluded the development of jaw bones, gill covers, scales and paired fins. Instead of the usual upper and lower jaw bones, they have a round suctorial mouth. Its inner lining and the tongue are covered with horny spikes used in their parasitic feeding. The hosts are other, usually larger, fish and the Lampreys first attach themselves with the sucking circular lip. The tongue is then used to rasp into the flesh of the host as the Lamprey feeds on it. Occasionally such a number of these parasites attach themselves to the host that they cause its death.

Both the Sea and River Lampreys normally spend their adult life at sea, though there is evidence that some River Lampreys spend all their lives in fresh water. The smallest species (about the size of a pencil) is the Brook Lamprey (*Lampetra planeri*), which never makes the migration to the sea and is found only in the upper reaches of rivers.

All three species have similar spawning habits. They ascend to the fresh water of the rivers and prepare a 'nest' on the sandy gravel bottom. To do this they remove pebbles with their mouths, usually dropping them downstream of the nest; it is not clear whether this is simply to get them out of the way or whether it is to protect the eggs by building a retaining wall. Once the eggs are laid and fertilised, they are covered with sand. The River Lampreys often make communal nests with up to twenty pairs combining, but the other two species work in isolated pairs. The eggs hatch into a larval form called a pride. The larva's mouth is slit shaped, the eye almost invisible, and the site of the future seven gill slits is marked by a groove; the animal lives in mud-banks more like a lugworm than a fish. This larval stage usually lasts some three or four years, after which the fish take up their swimming existence.

In the old days, Lampreys were considered a delicacy and almost every schoolboy knows that Henry I died of a surfeit of them. They were normally caught, at night, in eel baskets or nets, but the prides were dug out of the mud like worms and caught by hand. By the middle of this century they were becoming far less common and it seems likely that, again, some form of pollution was the cause.

This abundance of fish life on Sedgemoor has always been tapped by man. In the past it was largely for food and, especially near Glastonbury, a number of fishponds were created. Nowadays the stress is on fishing as a sport. The Huntspill River (New Cut) and King's Sedgemoor Drain are particularly popular; as well as the reservoirs, which have been stocked, especially with Trout,

Fishing for eels.

to increase the fishing facilities. Local youngsters still go eel fishing: a number of worms are tied together into a 'worm ball' or rayball. This is lowered into the water on the end of a piece of string or wire tied to a long stick. The eels are attracted to the worms and their bites are felt as vibrations along the 'rod and line' or as visible movements of the 'line'; there is no float. Once the eels are feeding, the line is swung on to the bank and, with luck, the eel is pulled out with its teeth still sunk into the worms. Very probably this method of fishing is as old as Sedgemoor itself.

The amphibia

The amphibia, as distinct from amphibious animals, are the vertebrates which start life as eggs laid in water, hatch into 'tadpoles' and then, as adults, can live on land. Frogs, toads and newts make up the British list.

Sedgemoor has always provided the ideal habitat for this group. The open, still water with its associated plant life gives the conditions needed by the female for laying her eggs. The plants and small water animals provide food for the tadpoles and the ditch banks and wet fields give the adults food, moisture and protection.

The eggs are laid in early spring, sometimes as early as February. Certain areas seem to be selected each year; sometimes one part of a ditch will be thick with eggs while another apparently identical stretch will be ignored; it is not known what governs

The Common Frog.

the choice of area. Frog spawn is laid in the great masses that everyone knows; in the process, the jelly mass absorbs water and swells so that a frog whose body is little larger than a hen's egg produces a mass of spawn which will fill a jam jar. The eggs are fertilised externally by the male; presumably the habit of the adults of gathering together ensures that the majority of the eggs are fertilised. While frog spawn floats in masses, toad spawn is laid in ropes; typically these are made up of a double row of eggs. Newt eggs are fertilised before laying, the female taking the gelatinous mass of sperms into her body first. They are laid singly and attached to the leaves of water plants, which are then folded over to protect the eggs.

The frog on Sedgemoor is the Common Frog (*Rana temporaria*). By July and August, places as different as a Westonzoyland garden and Shapwick Heath are alive with them. Large tadpoles and small frogs are carnivorous and form an important link between the small invertebrates which they eat and the larger animals which eat them. During her lifetime a female frog will lay several thousand eggs. If she lays 10,000, then 9,998 must die before they reach maturity, normally providing meals for their predators. This leaves the pair necessary to continue the species and keep the population constant.

The Common Toad (*Bufo vulgaris*) and the Natterjack (*B. calamita*) are found on Sedgemoor; so are the three species of newt, the Crested Newt (*Molge cristata*), Smooth Newt (*M. vulgaris*) and Palmate Newt (*M. palmata*). It is difficult to estimate

The Palmate Newt. The fact that Amphibians lay their eggs in water and the adults' prey is usually found near water, makes the Levels a very suitable habitat for them.

their numbers since adult toads are very well camouflaged and tend to sit tight. Toads and newts are inclined to wander some distance from the water in which they started their life. In the larval stage, toad tadpoles and frog tadpoles are often indistinguishable, but judging from the numbers of eggs, frogs far outnumber toads. Newt eggs are very difficult to find but larval newts can be distinguished since they retain their external gills (and tail) long after the legs have developed. Newts are quite common, two hundred yards of ditch probably yielding about half a dozen. During the breeding season when their colours are at their brightest and the crests of the males have developed, newts have a prehistoric look about them and seem very much a part of old Sedgemoor.

The reptiles

Only four species of reptiles occur on Sedgemoor and only the Grass Snake (*Tropidonotus natrix*) is at all common. This is the largest British snake, the females growing up to about 4ft long and the males about 3ft. Its general colouring is olive-green, with two crescent-shaped yellow patches behind the head. The best time to see them is on a warm day in spring when they come out to sunbathe on a stone or, more usually, a patch of bare earth. Amid lush vegetation they are very difficult to find. If they are disturbed, their normal reaction is to glide to the nearest ditch and swim away. Though this gets them away from human danger, it does make them easy to see and one can only assume that it is a fairly recent development in their behaviour. Presumably snakes have learnt to fear humans and 'realised' that a ditch provides a good defensive barrier. If they are eventually cornered, they will hiss and go through striking actions but their chief defence is the obnoxious secretion which they can give off.

The Adder (*Vipera berus*) is much less common and the peat moors are the only area in which it is likely to be found on Sedgemoor. It is distinguished by the black zigzag which runs along its back. The black lines are the same width as the spaces between the pinnules of a bracken frond; on a dead bracken frond, the pale brown pinnules are separated by dark spaces. An adder, coiled beneath it, exactly reproduces this pattern and very nearly reproduces the colours.

During the summer the adults feed on a variety of small mammals, lizards and newts. In the autumn they seek shelter, often among the peat blocks, and go into a form of hibernation before re-emerging the following spring. Because of its poison, the adder is, in a sense, a dramatic animal, but its limited numbers and the relatively small amount of food it takes do not give it an important place in the ecology of Sedgemoor. The Slow-worm (*Anguis fragilis*) and the Common Lizard (*Lacerta vivi-*

Grass Snakes are still reasonably common on the Levels.

Adders can sometimes be seen warming themselves on dry blocks of peat.

para) are present, particularly on the peat moors, but do not play a large part in the food webs.

The mammals

Broadly speaking the mammals fall into four groups. In terms of population, the largest group is that consisting of the small rodents such as mice and voles. These animals are mostly vegetarian, feeding on fruits, seeds, grasses and so on. In this group the small insectivorous shrews can be included. A fairly simple pattern is followed, whereby the climate and, later, the drainage affect the plants, which in turn affect the vegetarian rodent population. The shrew is 'one removed' in that the plant growth affects the insects on which it feeds:

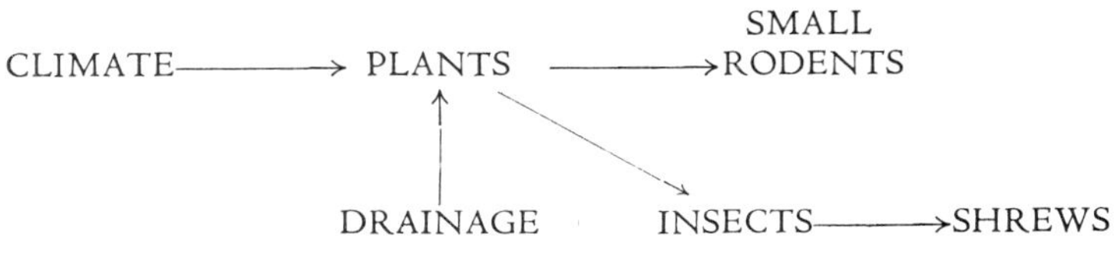

The rodent–shrew population, in its turn, provides food for the second group, the carnivores. These are mostly mammals, such as fox and weasel; but rodents are also taken by birds of prey, owls and snakes. Not only is there competition between these carnivores to catch their small rodent prey but a certain amount of limited inter-predation between members of this group; the larger carnivores feeding on the smaller ones. A fox will not only take mice and voles, but also a young stoat, a large beetle and a certain amount of vegetable food.

The third group comprises the large herbivores, the deer. As youngsters they may fall prey to the carnivores but once they have survived this stage they are likely to live until old age or disease cause their death. How much the large and small herbivores are in competition is not clear. Both deer and rodents are selective feeders, ie they do not feed on any available plant but select certain species.

The fourth group of mammals is headed by man and includes a few other omnivores, such as the wild boar, and the large number of herbivores which he has introduced. As far as Sedgemoor is concerned, it is only within the last two centuries that man and his animals have dominated the area.

The Short-tailed Vole is typical of the small mammals living amongst the grass stems.

The small mammals

Just as man has successfully invaded Britain, usually from the south-east, and driven across the country northwards and westwards, so have the voles and mice. Sometimes these invasions have been made by different subspecies and the terminology has become very complex. For the sake of convenience, reference is made here to three species of vole: the Bank-vole (*Clethrionomys glareolus*), the Short-tailed Vole (*Microtus agrestis*) and the Water-vole (*Arvicola amphibius*), and four species of mouse: the Long-tailed Field-mouse (*Apodemus sylvaticus*), the Yellow-necked Field-mouse (*A. flavicollis*), the Harvest-mouse (*Micromys minutus*) and the House-mouse (*Mus. musculus*).

Voles have a rounded head, small eyes and ears, and a shortish hairy tail. The Water-vole (often called a Water-rat) is clearly larger than the others; the chief distinction between the other two voles is their teeth shape, but the Short-tailed Vole also has a shorter tail, greyer fur and the ears are completely hidden. The vole's diet is almost entirely of grass and it lives either on or just below the ground surface. Despite its name, the Bank Vole often climbs around in hedges and is less selective in its feeding. The Short-tailed Vole is the really common one on Sedgemoor, according to the evidence of their habits and bird-pellet recovery. It is impossible to estimate the numbers or the amount of food they eat, but when an area is suddenly flooded the retaining banks can only be described as 'alive' with refugee voles.

The larger Water-vole is also common; on many parts of the moor, its holes average about one per yard of ditch bank. It feeds on a variety of the more succulent water plants and in a very small way holds the plants in check. They are very shy and one is more likely to hear a 'plop' as they dive into the water than to see them.

Again from the study of their habits and the recoveries from bird pellets, it seems that the Long-tailed Field-mouse is the most common mouse on Sedgemoor. The remains of Harvest-mice have also been recovered from bird pellets, but they are very few in number. It is impossible to estimate the numbers of mice, but there is little doubt that, together with the voles, they make up the bulk of the food taken by carnivores.

Three species of shrew occur on Sedgemoor; the Common Shrew (*Sorex araneus*), the Pygmy Shrew (*S. minutus*) and the Water Shrew (*Neomys fodiens*). Evidence shows that their populations are in the ratio of ten Common Shrews to one of each of the other two species. The Water Shrew is the largest of the three, between 3–4in long, and has a longer tail. Its feet show an interesting parallel with many aquatic insects: the digits are bordered with stiff hairs to increase the surface area and make them more efficient swimming organs. Its diet consists of a mixture of water insects (caddis fly larvae are often taken), snails, worms and small amphibia. Much of the feeding is done in the water but they have been found some distance away, presumably supplementing their diet.

A larger rodent now widespread is the Brown Rat (*Rattus norvegicus*). Not only does it directly compete with man, but it carries diseases which can be transmitted to man. This rat did not arrive in England until the beginning of the eighteenth century but, being hardier than the Black Rat (*R. rattus*), it extended its range outside the ports and spread across the whole country. Since rats are omnivorous, they can always find food and, with a high reproductive rate, rapidly become a menace. The pastures of Sedgemoor are not seriously threatened by this animal, which tends to thrive in grain-growing areas.

The Rabbit (*Oryctolagus cuniculus*) and the Hare (*Lepus europaeus*) both occur on Sedgemoor, the rabbit usually being found on the drier hill slopes around the moors, as wet ground is unsuitable for burrowing. The present pattern on the Levels of roughish pasture and relative freedom from man's interference suits the hare, which is a common sight in spring when the males go through their 'mad March hare' phase. The young are born in forms—nest-like depressions in the grass—and during the female's absence rely on their colouring and stillness for protection. Before she leaves them, the mother usually licks their fur the 'wrong way', so that instead of a sleekness which may reflect sunlight it becomes ruffled to increase the cryptic effect.

The carnivores

The wild boar, wild cat, marten and polecat have all been identified from the lake village site but none is still living in the area. Wolves and bears were almost certainly once present on Sedgemoor, but the only large carnivores to survive in any number are the Fox (*Vulpes vulpes*), Badger (*Meles meles*) and Otter (*Lutra lutra*).

Some foxes live completely on the moors, but the general pattern seems to be for them to have their dens on the hills around the Levels and use the moorland as a feeding area. Most of the year they are largely ignored, but during the winter tend to raid the villages. As a result, a number are shot each year. Sedgemoor is not a fox-hunting area.

Badgers, too, have their setts on the surrounding hills and descend to the moors to feed. Like rabbits and moles, badgers cannot dig into wet ground without the chambers becoming waterlogged. In 1955, however, one sow badger built a 'nest' of dried grass and reeds on the moor near Westonzoyland. It was about 2ft in diameter and almost the same height. Signs around it suggested that she had first tried to dig out a burrow but had been defeated by the high water table. She had built the 'nest' as an alternative and used it to rear her cubs successfully. This is the only recorded instance of this type of behaviour.

Stomach-content analysis shows that plants form a large part of a badger's diet. Beetles, worms and slugs are also eaten and, before myxomatosis, so were young rabbits. This relatively soft diet does not require highly specialised dentition or powerful jaw muscles, yet the badger has both. The muscles from the lower jaw do not end, like ours, near the temples; they continue as a thick band over the top of the skull and meet at a ridge in the centre. The teeth and musculature are what one would expect in an animal which followed larger predators and then fed on their leavings. An ability to crack bones would be an advantage since most of the large carnivores feed only on the more fleshy parts of their prey. When the larger animals became extinct, this source of food was no longer available to the badger and it was forced to change its diet. This theory suggests that the jaw muscles are vestigial and will probably decrease in size. That they are still so massive points to the fact that this change has happened—in evolutionary terms—fairly recently.

It is very difficult to estimate the number of otters on Sedgemoor, partly because of the distances they cover: they are reputed to travel twenty miles in a night. Recoveries from the lake villages indicate that otters were once quite common. In an area free of man's interference and with a plentiful supply of fish, a high otter population was very probable. This population may have dropped only slightly until the end of the eighteenth century, when man's influence would have accelerated the decline in the numbers of otters on the moors. This would have been due to disturbance of the habitat, as well as some killing for sport.

Otter tracks, with the widely spaced claws and partially webbed feet are all that, nowadays, most people ever see of these shy animals.

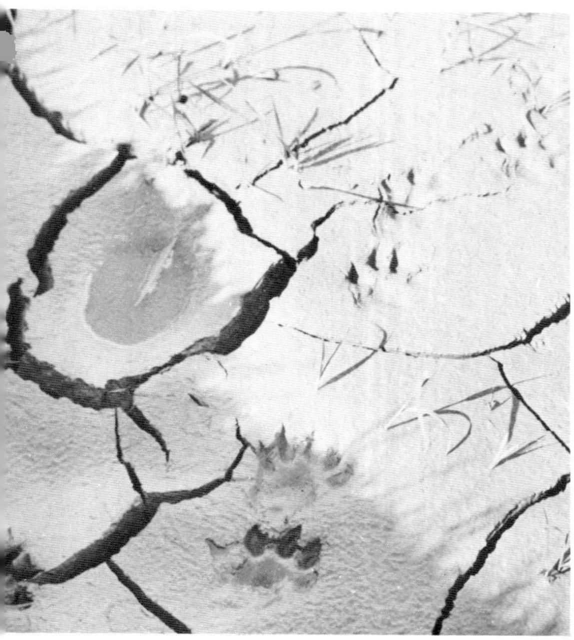

Two photographs of otters. Otters were once common on the Levels. Now their numbers are very much reduced and instead of being hunted they are protected.

Stoats (*Mustela erminea*) and Weasels (*M. nivalis*) are both fairly common; my own observations suggest that weasels outnumber stoats by about six to one. Except in game preserves, neither of these small carnivores has been heavily hunted, and their population has established a natural balance. In general, it follows that of the small rodents and fluctuates with theirs. This is particularly true of the weasel, as its diet is rather more restricted than that of the stoat, which often hunts along a river bank and takes eels or other fish which come within reach.

Feral mink have now become established on Sedgemoor.

The large herbivores

Two large herbivores appear in the old records: Red Deer (*Cervus elaphus*) and Roe Deer (*Capreolus capreolus*) occur in the lake village finds; today Sedgemoor has a small resident deer population. Occasional sightings indicate that herds sometimes move across the moors, though the species are rarely identified. It is surprising how well hidden deer can remain, especially in a thinly populated area like Sedgemoor. About the end of the 1950s, a Chinese

Muntjac (*Muntiacus reevesi*) was shot near Yeovil—one of the tiny deer introduced to England, which escaped from a private park and spread across the southern counties. Until this shooting, the Muntjac's presence was not known; it could have been the only one in the area or one of a herd.

One largish rodent herbivore which has completely disappeared is the Beaver (*Castor fiber*). It was present on Sedgemoor in the late Iron Age and became extinct in Britain about the fifteenth century. The reasons for its decline are not known. There were no significant climatic changes that affected it, nor were any predators introduced. The beavers would have been hunted for their skins and this, coupled with the destruction of their dams during early attempts to drain the Levels, probably led to their extinction.

Man and his animals

Ever since Sedgemoor was first populated, man has brought his domestic animals with him. In the past, Sedgemoor was treated as common land and eventually various rights were established. However, the grazing was poor and flooding limited access for a considerable part of the year. This intermittent grazing had relatively little effect on the moor and only in this last century have the cattle become so important. Man has turned much of Sedgemoor into pasture; the water table is adjusted to encourage grass for grazing and the whole economy is now geared to milk production. This concentration on creating an ideal habitat for cattle has meant in most cases a decrease in the variety of wild life. Fifteen wild mammals and six domestic ones were identified from the lake villages; bones found in similar circumstances today would be almost exclusively those of cows, mice and voles.

Portable milking parlours were extremely useful when farmers had fields scattered over a wide area. They have become quite scare within the last few years.

8

Bird Life

Sedgemoor holds a wide variety of habitats for birds: its wildness makes a suitable hunting ground for buzzards; its insect population means food for warblers and wagtails; its soft ground and rich soil fauna is ideal for waders, and the open water provides a feeding place for duck.

Whilst there is a certain amount of inter-specific predation among the birds, in general they are at, or near, the end of the food web. In some cases, they even deplete the potential food supply of the moor. For instance, herons nest in the woods surrounding the Levels, which means that, during the breeding season, fish taken from the moors eventually finish as the droppings which are ultimately recycled into the woodland trees. This loss to the moorland food supply is probably more than counter-balanced by debris from the hills, which gets washed on to the Levels.

For birds to breed successfully, they need food, nesting sites and, in many cases, suitable cover and freedom from interference. During the past two hundred years, these last three factors have all decreased and though bird life is still plentiful a changed pattern has become evident. This is chiefly apparent as a move from natural marsh to ditches and from open pools to man-made reservoirs.

While most species have survived this change of habitat, some have disappeared. Among the bones found around the lake village sites, those of the Dalmatian Pelican have been identified in sufficient numbers for it to be assumed that the birds were not just stray vagrants. Since they are now a species of south-east Europe, some large-scale change must have occurred. The likeliest explanation is that a period of cold weather had the ultimate effect of reducing the fish population as well as causing the death rate of the pelican chicks to rise considerably.

Remains of the White-tailed Sea Eagle and the Common Crane have also been identified from the lake village sites. Although these birds still occur as vagrants, it is reasonable to suppose that they were once far more common and have also suffered a habitat change.

In surveying the position of the birds on Sedgemoor, three main points emerge. Firstly, birds which originally used the flood water now use the reservoirs; not only do the reservoirs act as an alternative but, since they are permanent, they are attracting a

*The latest information on bird populations can be obtained from *Somerset Birds*, the annual report published by the Somerset Ornithological Society.

larger population. Secondly, as the drainage improves, so there is more pasture, which is of a semi-permanent, if not permanent, nature, providing a feeding ground for a number of species originally unknown or scarce on the Levels. Thirdly, there are those birds which need an open marshy habitat, space and seculusion; some of them have moved to the shallows of the reservoirs, but in most cases their populations have dropped considerably.

Birds may use several habitats within the course of their lives; a duck needs open water for its food supply, a drier habitat for nesting and it may also be involved in migratory flights. However, it is possible to divide the bird population into three groups: those mainly associated with open water; those associated with marshland and those whose chief habitat is the open pasture.

Birds of the open water

Before the drainage of the Levels, the natural open pools were fringed with rushes and sedges, and probably contained islands with a reed-swamp type of vegetation. Usually the moors did not flood until January or February. Now, there are large reservoirs around the borders of Sedgemoor, with relatively 'tidy' banks and providing permanent stretches of water where birds can settle at any time of the year. This adjustment to changes in the habitat means that, although the list of species remains much the same, the respective populations have fluctuated considerably.

Some seven species of wild duck occur fairly frequently on Sedgemoor.

WIGEON (*Anas penelope*) are winter visitors and, before the moors were drained, probably outnumbered all the other species put together; at least more were caught. During the middle of the last century, their numbers declined, probably because of improved drainage; they now average between 4,000 and 5,000 in February. Most of these birds are counted on the reservoirs, but in 1960 there was an exceptional count of about 5,000 birds on the flooded Wet Moor. These ducks are about the same size as the Mallard, but the males are generally grey with a very prominent yellow stripe down the centre of their dark brown heads. This stripe often shows when the birds are so far away that other markings cannot be seen. Perhaps its most unusual characteristic is its call; it does not quack, it whistles. Although occasional pairs have been seen late in the year, there is no definite evidence that they breed here. The vast majority leave in February–March and breed in northern Britain and Scandinavia.

TEAL (*Anas crecca*) replaced Wigeon as the commonest decoy

catch by the middle of the last century. This smallish duck is another winter visitor, numbering about three thousand; roughly a thousand of these live on flood water, while the rest of the population are found on the reservoirs. Some of the reservoirs have a few stands of reed-sedge vegetation and, as teal have a habit of resting in cover at the water's edge, it would seem that they have benefited from this establishment of permanent water and a little suitable cover. The winter Teal population has increased. Unlike the Wigeon, a few pairs have bred, but in general there is a migration towards the north-east in spring.

MALLARD (*Anas platyrhynchos*) are present on Sedgemoor throughout the year, in the same sort of numbers but seen far more frequently, being more active. During the winter they spend part of the day on the coast, especially on the Parrett Estuary, and then fly inland in the early evening to feed on the Levels. The old conditions, offering both feeding and nesting areas, were ideal for them, but with improvements in drainage their numbers decreased and by 1900 their population was quite low. With the establishment of reservoirs, the Mallard recovered and with the addition of migrants, the winter total is now about three to four thousand. Some of these breed by the reservoirs, but probably about a hundred pairs breed on the Levels. The nest sites are variable, ranging from tufts of sedge to hollows in pollarded trees. The junction between a broad rhyne and smaller ditch is often chosen, presumably because the first offers a good food supply and the second gives cover to the young ducklings.

POCHARD (*Aythya ferina*) are mostly winter visitors, with an average peak population of about one and a half thousand. In general colouring they resemble Wigeon, but the drakes have no yellow head stripe. This duck uses the flood water (about a thousand were counted on Wet Moor), but its population has only been appreciable since the reservoirs were built. The birds arrive in October–November and establish themselves on the reservoirs, needing a more permanent stretch of water than the floods provide. They then visit the flood waters when conditions are suitable. There is no evidence that Pochard breed here.

The PINTAIL (*Anas acuta*) is perhaps our most elegant wild duck. The drake's head and the back of its neck are chocolate brown, the breast and front of the neck a contrasting white; the body is a pearly grey. The Pintail has the long pointed tail which gives it its name. It is slender and long-necked compared with other species; a very elegant bird. The general pattern seems to be one of feeding on the Levels, and roosting on flood water or reservoirs. The winter population totals about five hundred. A few remain behind in the spring, and it has bred locally.

The SHOVELER (*Anas clypeata*) has a distinct spatulate bill and its typical swimming attitude is with the head partly lowered, so that the tip of the bill is only just clear of the water. The drake is

The Mallard duck is well camouflaged on its nest.

brightly coloured with a metallic green head, yellow eyes, white breast, brown flanks and black-and-white back and tail. The pre-drainage population is difficult to estimate, but seems to have been small, with a handful of breeding records. Like the Pochard, the Shoveler needs more permanent waters, as provided by a reservoir, to see it through the winter period; it is noticeable that when the flood waters have persisted for a longer period than usual, the Shoveler flocks have built up. Like the Pintail, the average winter population appears to be several hundred.

TUFTED DUCK (*Aythya fuligula*) occur in similar numbers. This black-and-white duck, looking like a schoolboy who cannot keep his hair down, follows the same pattern as the Shoveler and Pintail. Though the old marshy areas provided the necessary cover for the few which bred, the flood water was too impermanent to attract the large numbers which have probably only occurred since the reservoirs were built.

Goldeneye (*Bucephala clangula*), Garganey (*Anas querquedula*), Gadwell (*Anas strepera*), Scaup (*Aythya marila*), Common Scoter (*Melanitta nigra*), Smew (*Mergus albellus*), Red-breasted Merganser (*M. serrator*) and Goosander (*M. merganser*) have all been recorded from the Levels; but in very small numbers, apart from the Smew which has built up a largish reservoir population (about five hundred during the winter).

Seven species of goose have been recorded from Sedgemoor; all except the White-fronted Goose and the Canada Goose are rare and the inland records refer to irregular sightings of very small groups.

The WHITE-FRONTED GOOSE (*Anser albifrons*) usually arrives in late December or early January and the largest roost (its numbers may vary over the years from thirty to a thousand) is established around Steart in the Parrett Estuary. From here they fly inland to feed on the Levels, occasionally going as far south as Muchelney, but usually feeding on North Moor or Curry Moor. Wild geese are notoriously shy of human beings and these two moors are presumably chosen because they are quiet. The lake village finds show that Grey Lag and Bean geese visited the area in those times. It is likely that the winter population of geese has steadily declined as Sedgemoor has become less and less of a wilderness.

The GREBES (*Podiceps* spp) are represented in Somerset by six species, but only the Little Grebe (*P. ruficollis*) has used Sedgemoor to any extent. Like most of the true waterbirds, its population has increased with the opening of the reservoirs. Some of the birds are resident but the majority are summer visitors, the population reaching its height of about four hundred in August–September.

The MUTE SWAN (*Cygnus olor*) is, like the Little Grebe, described as 'locally common'. It was once considered a delicacy and there are records of the numbers eaten at banquets. There are references

The graceful Mute Swan is a resident on the Levels and can be seen over the whole region.

to a swannery at Wedmore and another at Meare Pool. By the middle of the last century, swans were described as widespread. In a 1955 survey, out of 126 nests, 72 were on lakes, ponds, rhynes, ditches and marshes; and 35 were on the rivers. There is now a small swan population on most of the reservoirs.

BEWICK'S SWAN (*Cygnus bewickii*) is a much less common winter visitor. It has a yellow-and-black bill and is slightly smaller than our native Mute Swan. It seems likely that this swan came to Sedgemoor in the hard winters, as it does now. Arriving in January, many birds go first to the flood water, the area around Langport being the most popular.

The MOORHEN (*Gallinula chloropus*) is widely spread over Sedgemoor. Typically they are seen in the larger rhynes or feeding in the fields. The noticeable thing about them is their timidity; in ornamental waters in towns, they are quite unconcerned about human beings, yet on Sedgemoor at the least disturbance they move into the sedges and skulk there. The young chicks resemble small bundles of black feathers and sometimes it is only when they are moving against the wind or water currents that one recognises them for what they are. Despite their very small size, the chicks are quite good swimmers and soon venture away from the parents. If danger threatens, they quickly return, clamber on board the parent and hide amongst its feathers.

The KINGFISHER (*Alcedo atthis*) is such a vivid bird that the occasional sightings remain firmly in one's mind. The Kingfisher's ideal habitat has clear water, an adequate number of smallish fish, a perch from which it can see them and mud banks in which it can nest. The larger rivers and drains on Sedgemoor have the necessary fish supplies, but their water is often muddy and the rivers are only suitable above their tidal limits. The water in the smaller ditches is often clear enough, but the numbers of fish are small; also, the plant succession occurs in the ditches, so they become less suitable as a habitat. With little or no water current, these small ditches are likely to become frozen over and are useless in very cold weather. In the severe winter of 1962–3, nearly all the open water was covered in ice for several weeks and, being unable to feed, the Kingfisher suffered badly. Since then its numbers have recovered to some extent, but the bird remains rare and is more likely to be seen nowadays on the reservoirs or the flooded brick pits of the coastal region.

OSPREY (*Pandion haliaetus*) bones were identified (though not with certainty) from the Meare lake village site. At the end of the last century there is a record of it from the woods overlooking West Sedgemoor. In the last thirty years there have been three sightings in the Sedgemoor area. This may indicate that the Osprey sometimes uses Sedgemoor in its migration flights. But the earliest record, though uncertain, does pose the question as to whether or not this fish-eating hawk was once a resident. The

Kingfishers are now uncommon but there are several records showing that they have built nests in the banks cut when peat is being extracted.

presence of the Osprey and the Pelican conjures up a wonderful picture of what the bird life of Meare Pool may have been like over two thousand years ago.

The SHELDUCK (*Tadorna tadorna*) is not really a Sedgemoor bird, though its bones have been identified from Meare and even now it occasionally breeds on the moor. The vast majority of the birds are coastal; until 1950 it was assumed that all the British Shelduck flew to an area off the coast of north-east Germany to moult (during their moult the birds are unable to fly). In that year two local ornithologists discovered that flocks, later found to average about two thousand birds, were using the waters of Bridgwater Bay during the moulting period. It was chiefly to protect these birds that a reserve has been established there.

Since Shelduck often use old rabbit burrows for nesting sites, it was feared that their numbers might decline when myxomatosis diminished the rabbit population. In 1961, the Warden of the Bridgwater Bay Reserve showed me a series of planks joined together like a child's toy railway-tunnel, about 5in high, 5in wide and 4ft long. I was told that they were rabbit burrows! Because of myxomatosis there were insufficient natural nesting sites for Shelduck on Steart Island; the Warden prepared artificial sites by digging scrapes in the ground, laying down his tunnels and then partially re-covering them. The experiment was successful; the 'burrows' were taken over by the Shelduck and used to rear their young.

The Heron is still widespread and it is rare to travel any distance over the Levels without seeing them.

Birds of the marshland

There is no clear-cut line separating the water from the marshy habitat; there is usually a band of 'in-between' vegetation. On the old Sedgemoor a marshy patch did not suddenly become a pool, the two blended into each other. On Sedgemoor today, a marshy field usually has a belt of plants growing half in and half out of the ditch which represents the water habitat. Seasonal and successional changes also occur; open water one month may become marsh by the next. Birds typical of the open water, such as duck, may roost or nest in the marshy vegetation. Others, like the Heron, stands among the marsh vegetation, reaching down to get its food from the open water. In some regions the term 'waterside' would be more relevant, but for the Somerset Levels the old word 'marsh' seems the most appropriate.

As the marsh habitat is becoming restricted to the edges of the ditches, it is there that Marsh Warblers and Reed Buntings are found. Resident waders like the Snipe are more likely to be by the side of a rhyne than in an open field. Winter flocks of some visiting waders can be seen searching through the wetter pasture, but these birds often commute between the Levels, the reservoirs and the coast. In general, smaller birds can still find all their needs in the marshy ditch fringe; but larger birds and those which occur in flocks are showing a population decline on Sedgemoor.

HERON (*Ardea cinerea*). If any bird can be said to typify Sedgemoor, it is the Heron, often called a crane locally. His grey solitary figure standing on the bank of a rhyne is as much a part of the Levels as are the withy trees and the autumn mists. A shaft of sunlight shows that he is not a dull, featureless bird, but an elegant one with black-and-white markings; the drab old man becomes the flashing young blade. He also seems to exemplify the timelessness of the moors; while the populations of his contemporaries have declined, he gives the impression that he has always been here.

Because of the Heron's habit of building nests in tall trees, as in a rookery, it is relatively easy to estimate its numbers. After the hard winter of 1962–3, there was a general drop in the Heron population, but it has now recovered and is holding quite steady. In 1965 there were 143 nests in the heronries around Sedgemoor, and in 1968 there were 146. Not all the birds hunt exclusively on Sedgemoor, some of the nest sites overlook other suitable areas, but it seems very probable that about ninety per cent of the food comes from the Levels. The populations of the various heronries fluctuate from year to year, mostly due to tree-felling; some heronries are disused while new ones are established. The Somerton site has been in continuous use for at least a hundred years, while the Brent Knoll heronry is only fifteen years old. Somerton has lost its position as the largest heronry and been superceded by Swell Wood.

There are two major heronries and several smaller ones around the edge of the Levels. The number of breeding pairs indicate that 300 or more Herons use the area as a feeding ground.

What is not clear is whether each heronry has its own attached territory. Do the birds from Swell Wood have exclusive rights on West Sedgemoor or do the birds from the different heronries intermingle? The fluctuating numbers for any particular heronry may also indicate a seasonal movement; ringed recoveries show an even greater flexibility: a dead bird found at Catcott had been ringed in Sweden.

The food of the Heron is made up of fish, frogs and similar aquatic animals. In addition to this vertebrate prey, it takes large numbers of Swan Mussels; the empty shells can be seen on the banks where Herons have been feeding. When the open water was frozen over in 1963, three dead Herons were brought to me for examination. The crop of one was empty, but the other birds each held the remains of voles; it is not known whether these are part of the normal diet or whether they are only taken when other foods are in short supply.

Since 1825 there is one record of a Squacco Heron (*Adeola ralliodes*) and four records of Night Heron (*Nycticorax nycticorax*) being shot on or around Sedgemoor. It was this type of record which gave rise to the saying 'What's hit's history, what's missed's mystery'.

The BITTERN (*Botaurus stellaris*) is more often heard than seen; its deep bell-like boom is extremely difficult to locate. The nest is built among reeds; when disturbed the bird points its bill upwards and stretches out its neck. This attitude, combined with its streaky, dark and pale brown colouring, gives it excellent camouflage. As a result the number of definite sighting records is small; nevertheless, though rare, the bird can be counted as a fairly regular winter visitor. Before the mid-nineteenth century it was fairly common on part of Sedgemoor, which would then have provided an ideal habitat; it is likely that the Bittern population has gradually declined as the moors have been drained.

The HARRIERS (*Circus* spp) are all now classed as rare, though the Hen Harrier (*C. cyaneus*), Montagu's Harrier (*C. pygargus*) and the Marsh Harrier (*C. aeruginosus*) have all been seen on the Levels. The Marsh Harrier is usually associated with Shapwick Heath, while the other two species, which are known to have bred, are more frequently reported from the coastal districts. Apart from an identification of Montagu's Harrier bones from the lake village site, no records of Harriers exist until the middle of the last century. As with the Bittern, it is possible that, with a habitat which offered all they required, these birds, especially the Marsh Harrier, were commoner than they are now, but were simply not recorded.

The old pollarded willow trees provide ideal nest sites and feeding places for birds such as the Greater Spotted Woodpecker.

The REED BUNTING (*Emberiza schoeniclus*) looks like a sparrow which has been spruced up and given a clerical bib; its brown upper parts seem brighter, its head much blacker and it has a white collar broken in front by a black bib. Many of these buntings are permanent residents; the ditch vegetation provides them with nest sites and the seeds which make up much of their diet. During the breeding season the cock takes up a prominent perch, such as a gate post, a conspicuous branch or an old Marsh Thistle stem. From this, he 'sings' a monotonous 'tseek-tseek' song to declare his territory. This busy little bird is apparently unaffected by the changed pattern and, for the moment, a settled member of the community.

The GREEN WOODPECKER (*Picus viridis*) and the GREAT SPOTTED WOODPECKER (*Dendrocopus major*) are now resident and both are uncommon. Ten years ago it was unusual to be on the moors and not hear the call of the Green Woodpecker; the old records suggest that it was once quite common; but the Spotted Woodpecker, which has never been very common, has built up its numbers since the beginning of the nineteenth century. With the increasing mechanisation of ditch clearing and the tendency to drag out the willows which commonly lined the banks, the Woodpeckers have been deprived of both nest holes and a source of food, provided by these trees. With their loss has come a permanent drop in the woodpecker population.

The BEARDED TIT or REEDLING (*Panurus biarmicus*) is a very

colourful exception to the general trend of declining populations. There are only five records of these very handsome birds before 1965, but in that year there was a sudden invasion. A flock of about fifty birds was seen on the Chew Valley Reservoir, a few at Blagdon Reservoir and five below Brean Down. It is not known why this sudden irruption occurred or if it was an isolated incident. It would be delightful if these birds became regular visitors and even bred here, but it seems a very optimistic hope.

A number of WARBLERS visit the Levels each year, but since most species prefer a wooded habitat it is unlikely that the populations will stay constant. So far the Grasshopper Warbler (*Locustella naevia*) is well established in the carr of Shapwick Heath, and the Sedge Warbler (*Acrocephalus schoenobaenus*) still finds adequate cover and food in the reeds and sedges. The rarer Reed Warbler (*A. scirpaceus*) breeds on the peat moors and in some of the withy and reed beds; the even rarer Marsh Warbler (*A. palustris*) is still to be found occasionally breeding on parts of Sedgemoor.

WADERS are sometimes seen in large flocks, mostly on the reservoirs, but there seems little doubt that human activities have gradually reduced their numbers over this last century. In some cases, the birds seem dependent on the reservoirs; the Redshank (*Tringa totanus*), for instance, has only come into the area since these artificial lakes were built. If such late arrivals are excluded, then the waders can be divided into four groups; the winter visitors which use the moors for feeding; the spring visitors which use the moor for nesting; passage migrants which are present for a very limited time, and the permanent residents. Sometimes different individuals of the same species belong to all four groups, but to the ordinary observer these divisions give an idea of what to expect throughout the year.

The waders are very well adapted to marshy or muddy conditions. Their feet are long, spreading their weight over as large an area as possible; their legs are also long, enabling them to feed in shallow water without their bodies getting wet and cold. They also have long slender beaks, with which to probe into the soft mud and collect their invertebrate food. Adapted as they are, three main local habitats are available to them: the coastal flats, the shallows of the reservoirs and the marshy fields of Sedgemoor. The weather is an important factor which determines exactly where they will be found at any particular time. Low temperatures, when the inland mud is frozen, will drive them to the coast; rough weather on the coast will drive them inland; in general, they are more likely to be seen on Sedgemoor during the mid-December to mid-January period.

The GOLDEN PLOVER (*Pluvialis apricaria*) is fairly typical of the winter visitors. The flocks usually arrive in autumn and leave by mid-April. Their main feeding grounds are the coastal mud flats around the mouth of the River Parrett, but large flocks of up to

Sedge Warblers, as their name implies, do use the sedges and coarse Reed-grasses. They are widespread over the Levels.

Golden Plover are winter visitors coming here to feed in the wet fields.

To many people the Curlew is a symbol of wide open moorland. In the depth of winter they are more commonly seen on the coast but some stay to breed on the wilder parts of the Levels.

a thousand can sometimes be seen feeding on Sedgemoor. The area around Chedzoy and the Tealham–Tadham moors seems particularly popular with this species.

The CURLEW (*Numenius arquata*) is most commonly a spring visitor to Sedgemoor. It is possible that a few birds are resident, but the majority move from the coastal belt on to Sedgemoor at the beginning of the breeding season. Although the Levels provide all the requirements of the Curlew, there are no breeding records before 1900, and it is only in the last twenty-five years that it has become common. The most likely reason for this is the improved drainage; the critical factor might be that wet chicks were previously more likely to die of cold: even incubation would have been difficult on a wet soggy nest.

WHIMBREL (*Numenius phaeopus*), though very similar in appearance and habit to the Curlew, are rare. Often they are only on the Levels for a few days in late April and again in early September. Both birds have the same down-curved probing beak and streaky brown plumage; they are about the same size (the Curlew is slightly larger) and there is even a close resemblance in their call. These two birds illustrate the rule that no two species, however much they resemble each other, occupy exactly the same territory and have exactly the same feeding habits.

SNIPE (*Gallinago gallinago*) are resident birds, though their population is boosted by winter visitors and passage migrants. At one time they were so common that, between 1878–91, 1,300 birds were shot at Shapwick, and a local ornithologist, writing at the same period, did not describe the bird because 'they are so common in any of the Taunton poulterers'. This seems a definite case of the population decreasing as the drainage improved. Because the land is drier, there are fewer rushy fields as suitable nesting areas, and more humans and cattle to disturb the nesting birds.

RUFF (*Philomachus pugnax*) have suffered even more than Snipe. Although there is no direct evidence, it is reasonably certain that they bred on Sedgemoor before it was drained. The elaborate breeding plumage of the male gave this bird its name; the females are called Reeves. Two hundred years ago it would have been possible to watch their breeding display, during which the males parade around each other, their ruff feathers raised, showing themselves off. This parade is interrupted by battles which, though not pursued to the extent of an individual being seriously harmed, establish a pattern of dominance and seniority. Unfortunately, the Ruff too has been affected by the drainage–interference pattern and nowadays its population is limited to a handful of winter visitors and passage migrants.

Birds of the pasture

It is impossible to draw a hard and fast line between marsh and pasture: the marshy fields provide very rough grazing and are studded with rushes and sedges; pasture fields are grazed or cut for hay, and relatively free of rush clumps. For most birds, the pasture fields are feeding rather than nesting grounds.

Since the pasture fields are largely a product of improved drainage, it is likely that most of the birds seen there are relative newcomers. This does not mean that a species did not occur on Sedgemoor before the nineteenth century, but it was probably present only in small numbers. This is the reverse of the pattern of marshland birds, whose numbers are declining; those of the pasture birds are increasing. It is too dramatic to say that the Starling has replaced the Ruff, but that indicates the general trend in the pattern.

The STARLING (*Sturnus vulgaris*) is the common bird of the pastures. Occasionally enormous flocks are seen; I estimated one flock to be about ten thousand birds. In the garden these birds often appear cheeky, greedy or quarrelsome, but their behaviour on the moors shows a very different pattern. Once a flock has settled in a field they all move forward in the same direction, probing the ground as they go. Presumably because they get less food, the ones at the back fly over the flock and form a new front rank. This leapfrogging is a continuous process so that there is always a movement of birds from the back flying over the flock to become the new leaders. As these newcomers land they are accepted without the squabbles that one sees in the garden and the whole effect is of the Starling flock flowing smoothly and harmoniously across the field. At night they pack together in well-established communal roosts, which have been shown to have a temperature considerably higher than the outer air temperatures; this is obviously an advantage on colder nights.

LAPWINGS (*Vanellus vanellus*) are, at times, almost as numerous as Starlings; in winter especially one sees very large flocks of them. As they wheel in flight, showing their white underwings and then their dark upper parts, they make a most attractive sight. In spring these large flocks break up as the birds establish their breeding territory. It is then that they fly backwards and forwards over the chosen area giving out their characteristic 'peewit' call. This rather mournful call, so common over Sedgemoor, contributes to its special character. It is usually heard on the wilder parts of the moor, as normally Lapwings choose the rougher fields for nesting; the nest being a simple, lined scrape on the ground.

FIELD FARE (*Turdus pilaris*) and REDWING (*T. iliacus*) are winter visitors; both come to Sedgemoor in large numbers, flocks of between one and two thousand being common. The majority arrive in November and depart in March and April. Their food is a mixture of berries, particularly hawthorn, and pickings, presumably a mixture of seeds and small insects, from the pasture fields.

Vast flocks of winter Lapwing are still common and those that remain to breed are usually found on the damp pastureland.

Grey Wagtails can be seen throughout the year, insects providing much of their food.

The Kestrel or Windhover is still a common sight as it hangs searching for its prey.

The YELLOW WAGTAIL (*Motacilla flava flavissima*) is a summer visitor. It arrives as the Field Fares and Redwings are departing and normally takes up its territory fairly soon after arrival. Apart from the late summer roosts, it is not seen in flocks like the rest of the Wagtails; it seems to prefer an association with cattle so that it can feed on the disturbed insects. Its yellow plumage and flickering flight makes it as attractive a pasture bird as the Kingfisher is on the water. The Grey Wagtail (*M. cinerea*) is a resident and, because of its yellow rump, is sometimes confused with the Yellow Wagtail, though it is not so canary-coloured. The Blue-headed Wagtail (*M. flava flava*) is a rare passage migrant; it is distinguished by its head, which is blue-grey above the eye stripe.

The KESTREL (*Falco tinnunculus*) is the commonest bird of prey and it is unusual to spend an afternoon on the moors without seeing one. In many parts of the country the widespread use of insecticides has had a very harmful effect on this bird but, fortunately, the Sedgemoor farmers have not taken to much large-scale use of chemicals and the Kestrel population is relatively stable. It is not a marshland hawk, so it is very probable that, before the drainage schemes were established, the numbers of Kestrels were rather lower than the present figure.

The NIGHTJAR (*Caprimulgus europaeus*) is not strictly a pasture bird, belonging more to heath and woodland, but the heath on the peat moors is almost equivalent to the pasture on the fen. The bird usually comes to the district in mid–May and establishes itself in the carr–woodland area around Shapwick Heath. This area is relatively quiet, has plenty of nesting sites amongst the heather and bracken, and an abundance of insect food. The Nightjar is so well camouflaged that it is extremely difficult to see it in daylight. During the day it rests, often against a branch, and the best time to see it is in the dusk when it starts to feed. Usually the first sign of activity is its call, which has been likened to a two-stroke cycle engine. Its flight is a mixture of gliding and sudden quick darts after moths or other suitable insects. Though the flight movement is almost as quiet as an owl's, sometimes a sharp slap can be heard; this is made when the wings clap together. Whether the sound is accidental or has some significance—perhaps to disturb insects—is not known. The population is reasonably steady at the moment, but as more of the carr is removed for peat cutting inevitably the Nightjar will become scarcer. With such a limited breeding area on Sedgemoor, it is probable that it will soon be restricted to the surrounding hills.

The list on the following page, showing the species and numbers seen during two morning walks around Westonzoyland gives an idea of the birds which a visitor to Sedgemoor can expect to see.

	30 MARCH	20 AUGUST		30 MARCH	20 AUGUST
Blackbird	4	10	Partridge	2	—
Blue Tits	3	8	Pied Wagtail	2	—
Buzzard	2	—	Reed Bunting	8	2
Chaffinch	8	3	Robin	1	2
Chiffchaff	1	1	Rook	2	7
Crow	5	1	Sedge Warbler	—	1
Field Fare	35	—	Skylark	4	—
Goldfinch	—	3	Snipe	4	1
Great Tit	2	4	Song Thrush	—	1
Green Woodpecker	—	1	Spotted Flycatcher	—	1
Grey Wagtail	—	2	Starling	200	6
Hedge Sparrow	—	3	Swallow	—	2
Heron	1	1	Swan	5	—
House Sparrow	—	c150	Tree Creeper	—	1
Kestrel	—	2	Whinchat	—	3
Lapwing	c100	—	Whitethroat	—	3
Linnet	—	2	Willow Warbler	—	3
Magpie	7	8	Wren	1	—
Mistle Thrush	2	—			

As the old dry heath surfaces are becoming scarcer, so the population of Nightjars is declining.

9
Local Industries

Although Sedgemoor is principally a dairy-farming area, its formation and geographical position have led to the development of several specialised craft industries. None of these has been on a large scale, but they have provided jobs and, to some extent, shaped the landscape, helping to give the Levels their own special character.

Some of these crafts, such as withy growing, are almost as old as Sedgemoor itself; others, such as peat extraction, have their origins in man's first attempts to utilise the moors. They have recently expanded to such an extent that the early workers would scarcely recognise the methods now in use.

Unfortunately, the expanding local industry is the exception; many activities have either disappeared or are likely to do so in the near future. There are several reasons for this; cheap mass production, the widespread use of plastics, and the desire of young people to work in the light industries based on the larger towns.

Something of the old crafts is still in evidence on the Sedgemoor landscape: the lines of drying withies around West Sedgemoor, the peat ruckles of Shapwick and the flooded clay pits between Bridgwater and Highbridge give the area its individual character.

The kiln of an old brick works

Brick and tile works

Unfortunately the brick industry has suffered a setback; many of its buildings are now disused and being dismantled. Still to be seen are the pits from which the clay was dug. Most of them are now colonised by reeds, but sufficient open water remains for them to be popular with local anglers, and such water birds as the Great Crested Grebe. A number of rare migrant warblers have also been noted from these pits. Occasionally they are used officially as rubbish dumps, but it is to be hoped that this practice will be restricted, since the flooded pits make much-needed habitats for wild life.

The tile industry is more in evidence, however, since almost every building is roofed with its products. The varying patterns and shades of tile, complemented by the angles of the roofs, are an attractive feature of the local architecture. Because the climate is warm and damp, and the tiles retain some moisture, an untended roof soon becomes colonised with mosses and stonecrops; some of the old barns look particularly decorative.

Cob walls

The clay was also used in making cob walls. These were made of unbaked clay reinforced with stones and straw or similar binding material. A rendering of plaster was applied to the sides to make them weatherproof. A few of the old cottages still retain their original cob walls; these have no damp course, but since they are usually several feet thick they are very efficient insulators, keeping the cottage cool in summer and warm in winter. Regulations now prohibit the use of cob and, as many of the old buildings are modernised, cob walls are rapidly disappearing.

Pollarding

Most of the old willow trees which line the ditches are pollarded, ie they have been 'beheaded' about 8ft from the ground. A new head of straight branches grows out from this point and can be harvested when the branches are thick enough. These branches are used as hedge stakes, for hurdles, split-wood fencing, and the framework of some basket work. Many of these pollarded willows have now been grubbed out, partly because they impede mechanical ditch clearing and partly because the demand for the wood has declined.

West Sedgemoor is still the main withy growing area. The current year's growth is cropped whilst the stocks are left to produce next season's shoots.

Withy growing

Osiers, or withies, were probably used when men first inhabited Sedgemoor. The twigs are light, springy and more resistant to decay in water than most woods. This makes them particularly suitable for use out of doors, as lobster traps, farm hurdles or garden furniture.

As with other plants coming under cultivation, the wild stock has been improved; two varieties, Black Mole and Champion are particularly popular. Short cuttings are first planted in rows, some 17,000 to an acre. In the autumn, when they are rooted, they are pruned almost to ground level. These provide the stocks which, in the next growing season, will put out a number of long, straight shoots. These are harvested, the stocks being left to produce another crop of shoots for the following year. The

The rods being boiled to give them the appropriate colour.

Bundles of 'rods' awaiting further management.

The rods being woven into the finished article.

cut shoots or 'rods' are then 'managed'. The chocolate-brown colour is produced by steaming the rods while they still have their bark; the white ones have the bark removed while the sap is rising; and the reddish-brown tint is obtained by boiling them for a short while before stripping off the bark. The coal needed for the boiling and steaming was brought up to Sedgemoor by river and often the rods were carried out in the same way to be made up elsewhere.

At the beginning of the nineteenth century, withy growing was a comparatively large concern, centred around Stathe; something like £6,000 of willows were produced each year. This is one case where the improvement of drainage has not had any pronounced effect. Although withies grow well in damp ground, it does not have to be very wet and the trees will thrive on the moor as it is at present. The trade continued to be prosperous until fairly recently but, particularly in the last twenty years, it has declined. In the mid-1950s there were 4,000 acres growing withies, ten years later it was only 1,000 acres. Two factors brought about this decline. Firstly, the use of withies for clothes baskets, etc has largely been replaced by plastics; at Bridgwater fair it is easier and cheaper to buy a plastic clothes basket than a wicker one. The other factor is that young people prefer to work in light industry in towns like Taunton. At the moment with a slight increase in the number of visitors to the area and the current fashion for Victoriana and basket furniture, the industry is just about holding steady. A reviving public interest in 'natural' products and country crafts may be a hopeful sign for local withy growers.

Teasel growing

There is no evidence to show when teasels were first grown commercially. It is probable that there was a gradual move in that direction from harvesting the wild teasels. The plant is now recognised as having two subspecies: *Dipsacus fullonum sylvestris*, the wild form, and *D. fullonum fullonum*, the cultivar. The bracts on the receptacle of the wild variety are considered too flexible for use; those in the cultivated form end in a stiff recurved spine. These hooks are used to raise the nap on woollen cloth to give a softer feel. The woollen industries of south-west England and Yorkshire were the chief markets for teasel growers, but with the development of new techniques teasels are no longer required. A very small area around Fivehead is all that remains of what was a go-ahead concern.

Billingsley has left us an account of teasel growing at the end of the eighteenth century and, apart from changing prices, his description could apply to almost any period. He tells us that, although wild teasels are occasionally found on the acid peat moors, they do best in a rich soil and the area to the east of Taunton is

Bundles of teasels being harvested.

Two photographs of a cider press, one showing the press in operation with the apples packed between layers of straw.

particularly suitable for the cultivated variety. The seeds are sown in April and the weeds are kept down by hoeing with traditionally shaped long narrow spades. In the late autumn the biennial plants are thinned out and the thinnings are replaced. The cleaning and loosening of the ground is repeated some three or four times and the plants are earthed up by the following spring. Flowering occurs in July and the heads are ripe as soon as the blossom falls. The ripe heads are cut and tied into bundles for drying in the sun before sorting. The best quality are called Kings, the medium ones are called middlings and those unfit for use are the scrubs. When Billingsley was writing, 40s (£2) was the price for a peck of Kings, about 9,000 heads; the same amount bought about 20,000 middlings.

To get a good crop it is essential that the beds should be kept free of weeds. To encourage the men to work well a principle of profit sharing was introduced; a profit of £5 16s (£5.80) per acre for the two-year period was considered a good return.

Cider making

Until fairly recently, many farms and most of the local inns brewed their own cider. In the early nineteenth century a farm labourer received a gallon of cider for each acre of mowing grass that he cut. One still hears tales of men who drank several pints before the breakfast break and whose daily consumption was about two gallons during the working day, followed by more during the evening's social drinking.

The cider-apple orchards were usually on the slightly higher ground of Sedgemoor. Some of these old orchards are still standing; in Westonzoyland, for example, there are two left on the outskirts of the village, but half a dozen orchards within the village have been grubbed out and built over. Over the last ten years cider manufacture has been concentrated in a few large firms, which have their own well-cared-for orchards; the small local ones were no longer required. The trees were rarely pruned or treated and the crops tended to be haphazard.

Peat extraction

Though layers of peaty soils exist over much of Sedgemoor, it is only in the area north of the Polden Hills that the raised bogs formed to give deposits of workable peat. One deposit, running from Catcott Heath through Shapwick Heath to Glastonbury is just under four thousand acres and a second deposit to the north, around Westhay, covers a little over two thousand acres; a total of more than nine square miles. The oligotrophic conditions began in this area between 3,000 and 2,000 BC and

Some of the old tools used in cutting and carrying peat. Displays illustrating peat extraction can be seen at The Willows Garden Centre near Shapwick and at the Somerset Rural Life Museum, Glastonbury.

plants capable of growing in this poor acid soil became established. Sphagnum moss and associated plants grew well and led to the formation of the raised bogs, completely dependent on rainfall for their water supply. In these conditions minor climatic changes produce a relatively large response from the vegetation. In the wet periods, the sphagnum grows well and eventually produces a pale fibrous peat. In dry conditions, the sphagnum is superceded by ling, cotton grass, etc, which produce a dense dark humified peat. It is this dark peat which is valued as a fuel.

The average depth of the peat is now about 12ft. Above this is a thin layer of topsoil which carries the vegetation. Depending on man's activity, this ranges from heath, with sundew and orchids, to climax woodland. The water table varies seasonally, but is usually very near the surface.

The Westhay Moor deposit contains a high proportion of cotton grass. Since the remains of this plant are coarse and fibrous, it is more difficult to cut and mill. Once cut, the blocks are more likely to crack and break as they dry out. For this reason, peat cutting around Westhay has been on a restricted scale. The Shapwick deposits, on the other hand, have been extensively worked, especially over the last fifty years. It seems probable that as the Shapwick deposits are cut, so the costs of further removal will increase and at some point it will be economically worthwhile to open up the Westhay area. At the moment the two areas are distinct, but as work progresses they are more likely to be fused into one economic unit.

Until a hundred years ago, peat digging was a purely local concern. Common rights of turbary were in existence and the peat dug out was used for fuel. Commercial digging started about 1870. The use of peat in horticulture has gradually increased until, today, about ninety per cent of it is used in one branch or another of horticulture.

The traditional method of cutting the peat is with a hay knife and a special spade. The top vegetation is first cut and burned

The old method of digging peat by hand.

Peat being dried in stacks called ruckles.

Originally the peat was carted away and used as fuel. Nowadays it goes to nurseries and market gardens etc.

away and then the few inches of top soil are removed from a strip about 12ft wide. The hay knife is a large flat blade with a handle bolted to it at right angles. This is used rather like an enormous scalpel to cut into the peat. The spade is then used to take out pieces, called mumps, which measure 10in by 9in by 8in. These are stacked at the side of the trench until a 2ft layer of peat is removed. Since this would often bring the bottom of the trench below the water table, a pump is used while the peat is being worked. Once the peat is stacked, the pumping is discontinued and the trench usually fills with water. A special type of flat wheelbarrow is used to move the mumps away from the edge of the trench to a stacking area. First they are put into small stacks, called stooks, where they are left to dry. Once they have partially dried and contracted, they are re-stacked in larger heaps, called ruckles. These are made by arranging the blocks in a circle with a space between each block to allow air to circulate. Further rings are placed on top of the first one until the ruckle is about twenty mumps tall. Towards the top, the diameter of the circle of blocks is decreased so that a dome effect is produced. Eventually a ruckle looks like an enormous old-fashioned beehive. The whole drying process takes about a year.

Once it has dried, the peat can be sold in blocks for fuel or ground for use in horticulture.

Nowadays most of the cutting is by machine. The process is basically the same; the machine uses a blade like a spade which takes out a slice of peat about 3ft deep by 2ft wide and 6in thick. This is automatically cut into manageable pieces about the same size as the hand-cut mumps. The drying process is the same and then the peat is moved by light railway to the granulating sheds.

When an area is first opened up, the peat is removed in strips so that a series of 2ft deep trenches run across it. Topsoil from the newer workings is often dumped in the old ones but, apart from this, they are left.

These old cuttings do not form fresh peat; reedmace plants are usually the first to colonise them and then they follow the normal succession for the area. In fact the bogs ceased to be active by about AD 400 and since then no more peat has been made. The area is, therefore, being denuded of peat without any natural counterbalancing process.

The removal of peat is a rapidly expanding industry. If the present rate of increase is maintained, production in 1986 will be ten times as great as that in 1954. As the top layers of peat are stripped away, so the problem of water control becomes more acute; but the general improvement in drainage over the whole of Sedgemoor will have its effect on the cost of peat removal: the drier it is, the cheaper the extraction.

Once the peat has been removed, the hole rapidly fills with water. The water then becomes invaded by plants like the Reedmace (bullrushes) and these areas quickly become a haven for many kinds of wildlife.

10

The Future of the Levels

NOTE: These comments (pages 132 to 134) were written in 1971 for the first edition of this book. They made one of the first public airings of the potential problems of the Levels and were at least partly responsible for awakening interest in the area and for alerting people to the threats to the wildlife. They are retained here so that readers can make their own judgements as to their accuracy and decide whether or not they were justified.

It is often emphasised that England has very little natural landscape. Most of our scenery is the result of patterns of farming practice. This applies to Sedgemoor; its present appearance is due to the economic methods of dairy farming on this type of soil in this type of climate in the middle of this century. Only the climate is likely to remain fairly constant. With our entry into Europe, there will inevitably be changes in farming policy. Modifications in Britain's dairy production will doubtless be linked with the move towards bigger farms and, if not factory farming, at least more chemico-mechanical control. Advancing technology means that drainage of the Levels can be further improved and, if this happens, the lush green permanent pastures could be converted into arable land.

Already Sedgemoor is showing a move in this direction, more land is being ploughed each year and, although it is usually put down to cereals, potatoes and roots can also be grown very successfully.

Quite apart from external considerations, the enormous tie of a small dairy herd is being resented more with each generation of farmer. The present pattern of small fields lined with ditches is almost certain to disappear. Even those ditches which must remain may be converted into underground channels, as is already happening where they interfere with motorway construction.

Thus, from the farming point of view, much larger units carrying a variety of crops can be expected. In place of ditches, post and wire fences will divide the fields, and most of the trees and copses will be felled, so that the larger fields can be treated uniformly.

Local conservationists will doubtless oppose these changes, but it is unlikely that they will be able to withstand the pressures of an increasingly urban population.

Not only will the general appearance of Sedgemoor be altered, but the rate of disappearance of most of its unusual plants and animals will be increased rapidly. It is quite probable that more local nature reserves will be set up, but they will become progressively more costly. This is not only because the price of land is certain to rise but, as the drainage improves, special precautions would have to be taken to retain the old marshy conditions needed to support some of the wild life and organisms. Without technological assistance, one cannot maintain a marsh in the middle of dry ground. At present, the general policy is to try to establish a nature reserve to surround and protect unusual habitats and their flora and fauna. In the future it seems likely that reserves will have to be established where a habitat is either suitable or convertible. Plants and animals from other threatened areas will then have to be transplanted to new reserves. In the past the idea of transplanting rarities was considered to be ecologically unwise and a form of 'cheating'. Soon, it may be the only way in which they can be saved.

It may well be that the motorway will bring other changes to the area. Already there are discussions on the future of Severnside, the region covering the coast of the Bristol Channel from Bristol and Avonmouth down into Somerset. With a fast road-link with the remainder of Britain, it is expected that the area will develop and new light industries be introduced. It is already the site of a concentration of atomic power stations and, though industry is no longer closely linked with the geographical source of power, it seems likely that these stations are the forerunners of industries yet to come.

Very often nowadays the factor which controls industrial distribution is the available water supply. Those industries which do not need 'clean' water can get it from the Severn Estuary and there is always the possibility of a Severn barrage scheme being completed. This could be either a tidal barrage providing electricity or, more likely, a barrage primarily to trap fresh water on the landward side, with electricity production as a 'bonus'.

If such industrial expansion occurs, then there is the problem of the appropriate labour force. Several centres in the area have considered becoming over-spill towns, envisaging a movement from London. So far, this has not happened on any appreciable scale, but should there be an industrial demand for labour this situation could quickly change.

At present there is the phenomenon of over-spill villages. Over the last twenty or so years there has been a noticeable influx of people into this area. Although such towns as Bridgwater and Taunton have done a lot of house building, this has not absorbed the whole of the increase in population. Many people prefer to live in the outlying villages, resulting in an inevitable change in the pattern of village life. Up to about ten years ago newcomers entered the villages in ones and twos, and were absorbed into the existing life. Since then, the influx has been so rapid that the villages have changed from communities largely dependent on the surrounding land into those which are really dormitory suburbs of neighbouring towns.

Not only can a larger resident population be expected, but also an influx of casual visitors. Resorts such as Weston-super-Mare

are already geared to this, but with the motorway's quick and easy link to the Midlands, people living there will take the opportunity of driving down to Somerset for a few hours. This could lead to the familiar clash between the farmer who works the land and the visitor who wants car parks, access roads, open areas and picnic sites.

The railways too will probably play a part in the development, with the promised inter-city trains travelling at speeds of up to 150mph. This could lead to commuting on a much more ambitious scale. Many people dream of a cottage in the West Country. It may be practicable to live on Sedgemoor, use the motorway to Bristol and then catch a train to a job in London.

Although one cannot forecast the rate at which these changes will take place, the essentially rural character of Sedgemoor may soon be replaced by fewer but larger, highly mechanised farms, with more land used for housing and a clash between those who support a utilitarian land-use policy and those who want more areas set aside for leisure pursuits.

Policies affecting the whole area are exemplified on a small scale in the present discussions regarding the future of Shapwick Heath. It is confidently predicted that the extraction of peat will go ahead at a steadily increasing rate. Estimates vary, but somewhere between twenty and fifty years from now the whole of the peat will have been removed. In fact, even twenty years may be an overestimate.

When the Shapwick/Westhay cuttings are exhausted, a large hole covering about four square miles will be left. Even allowing for improved drainage, this excavation will fill with water and the present peat moors will become a large, fairly shallow lake. Theoretically, it could be filled in and converted to some other purpose, but the demand for water is so great that its use as a reservoir seems inevitable. Apart from providing a conventional water supply, proposals are already being put forward for subsidiary use of the reservoir. The first is that it should be the site of some form of marina, with facilities for sailing and water-skiing. This envisages its use by visitors from some distance away, using the motorway as access, and a need for restaurants, motels and other amenities.

The second scheme is based on using the water chiefly for fishing, also drawing visitors from a distance, but possibly seeking a quieter, less sophisticated environment.

The third proposal is to convert the water and its surroundings into a reserve for wild life. This would necessitate even fewer ancillary buildings, and the habitat would be conserved in as natural a way as possible.

However, the future Shapwick lake is going to be a large one, and there is no reason why it should not be divided into three areas, so that all of these schemes can be carried out and everyone's interests served.

Looking back at forecasts written some fourteen years ago, it is interesting to see what changes have actually taken place on Sedgemoor.

One change, which I regret, is that Sedgemoor has almost lost its name, Nowadays the homely 'countryfied' title has been replaced by the colder sounding 'The Somerset Levels' or sometimes 'The Somerset Levels & Moors'. This is partly due to a desire to avoid confusion with Sedgemoor District—an administrative area of the county, but I suspect that the loss of the original title is largely due to the uncertainty of nomenclature to which I referred in my original introduction.

As to what has happened on the land itself, certainly there has been a move towards intensive farming. The amount of arable land has increased year by year and technology has been used to increase the drainage of the Levels. Large scale flooding is becoming unusual and the land is being dried out much quicker, the old wet, rushy pastures are becoming scarcer every year.

More and more frequently ditches are being replaced by mole drains, other ditches are being deepened and kept 'cleaner' so that the fields can be dried out as soon as possible. All this is leading to a change in the character of Sedgemoor. Just as towns are becoming more and more alike, so the Levels are becoming more and more like any other part of farming Britain.

Until very recently Government policy was urging more and more milk production. To accomplish this many farmers were persuaded to plough up the original permanent pasture and replace it with selected grass/clover strains. This produced more milk but the loss of the permanent pasture also meant the loss of 'weeds' or the loss of a 'wealth of wild flowers, insects, birds etc.'—depending on ones point of view.

Meanwhile, some of the more far-seeing farmers were anticipating that this would result in a milk surplus and they were switching to arable farming.

Whilst these developments were taking place, the conservation movement was gathering a good deal of support and some of this support was coming from the farming community itself—some farmers are traditionalists and dislike change, they like the blend of farming and wild life that the earlier pattern had engendered, and even amongst the 'intensive' farmers were many who were looking for some way of improving their yield and yet leaving something of the wild life.

It was to try to resolve this problem that the Nature Conservancy Council (NCC) arranged a series of discussions and studies during the mid-seventies. This led to the publication of 'The Somerset Wetlands Project' in 1977. The studies indicated that there was no simple solution, it was not possible to intensify the farming methods and, at the same time, keep up the richness of the wild life. The paper then proposed a series of options ranging from the extremes (all for agriculture or all for conservation), to a land-use strategy suggesting that some areas should be designated for agriculture, others for peat extraction, conservation etc. Interested bodies were circulated and their comments sought. As was to be expected there were many reservations but the vast majority of those that replied felt that some land-use strategy avoiding either extreme was the best solution.

In the next few years there was a general feeling that the country's agricultural policy was misconceived and that it was leading to a widespread destruction of wild life in exchange for 'milk-lakes' and 'butter-mountains'. Certainly this was the impression given in the popular press. This was an over-simplification but it, along with more informed opinion, pressed the Government into action and the 'Wildlife & Countryside' Bill was passed in 1981. As far as Sedgemoor is concerned, this empowered the NCC to set up areas known as Sites of Special Scientific Interest (SSSIs). To qualify for such a designation the land must have a definite wild life value. Once land has been so designated then, briefly, any change in farming practice can only be carried out with NCC approval. Both farmers and conservationists argue that there are faults in the Act; the sooner these are ironed out the better and then, even if it goes against ones own ideas, at least everyone will know where they are and they can settle down again and start working together.

In 1984 it was realised by the designers of the Common Agricultural Policy (CAP) that Europe was overproducing in certain areas. As a result there is to be a considerable drop in milk production.

There seems to be three possible outcomes to this latest policy. Land now given over to dairy farming could be converted to arable, or there could be a general lowering in efficiency (rather unlikely) or more land could be farmed so that its wildlife is encouraged. In other words could not land be farmed not for cows or potatoes but for marsh orchids and snipe? Farmers obviously want to make a living but if they can be grant-aided to produce unwanted milk, then why not grant-aid them to support wildlife? This idea is not far-fetched, indeed farmers whose land is designated as part of an SSSI are already eligible for grants as a form of compensation. What I am suggesting is not so much a change in the financial rewards to farmers as a change in attitude. At the moment many farmers feel that they are being discouraged from farming 'properly'. I would like this to change to a more positive view where they are encouraged to farm for some wildlife and can take as much pride in having nesting Godwit or Green-winged orchids as in producing any

NOTE: In 1987 much of the Levels have been designated as an Environmentally Sensitive Area (E.S.A.). Farmers and land owners can voluntarily enter the scheme and be eligible for Grant Aid providing that they accept restrictions which, in effect, mean that they follow the traditional pattern of farming. Those farmers who have not modernised are expected to welcome this scheme and even those who have modernised some of their holdings may well be encouraged to take the E.S.A. offer on their as yet 'unimproved' land. If this scheme is widely taken up it will do much to safeguard the wildlife which is still to be found.

other crop. It is the psychological difference between compensation for poor farming and a reward for a farming/wildlife policy.

Whilst these discussions and policy statements have been going on at European and national level, the voluntary bodies have not been inactive. The Royal Society for the Protection of Birds (RSPB) now owns a significant part of West Sedgemoor, and the Somerset Trust for Nature Conservation (STNC) have bought land north of the Polden Hills, These have become Nature Reserves and details can be obtained from their respective headquarters. Establishing this type of Nature Reserve does not mean taking the land out of production, the land is still used for grazing and/or hay, it is simply a way of ensuring that the traditional patterns continue.

On the peat moors the rate of peat extraction boomed in the 60s and 70s but it now seems to have levelled off. Some of the land will almost certainly be set aside as a fresh water store and another area left 'empty' so that flood water can be pumped into it as the need arises. However, the large scale 'Avalon Lakes' scheme seems less likely to mature. One factor which has affected this is the possibility of keeping the land, albeit nine to twelve feet below its 1960s level, reasonably dry by pumping. This land can then be returned and farmed as 'low-level' agriculture.

Elsewhere on the peat land the STNC have established nature reserves. Some of these are on the original (1970s) surface and support the range of special peat moors wildlife. Other reserves are on the sites of the worked out peat beds and these small lakes and reed beds are already providing a valuable refuge. One reserve in particular has been set aside for experiments in management techniques and it has already yielded some valuable information. In effect, these are small scale experiments on farming the land to give a crop of wildlife.

The idea of a Severn Barrage scheme is still being mooted but the general slowing down of the country's economy has not led to any rapid expansion of the Severn side as a light industrial area. Whether an upsurge in the economic climate will revitalise these plans remains to be seen.

In today's paper (September 1984) there is a reminder that we have enough oil to last to the end of the century. It is almost impossible now to imagine life without oil, plastics and other oil products. What I wonder will Sedgemoor be like in the year 2000!

A typical view of the old traditional Sedgemoor. Increasingly these scenes are disappearing and being replaced by a 'tidied up' but far less interesting landscape.

Bibliography

Proceedings and Annual Reports of the Somerset Archaeological and Natural History Society

Andrewartha, H. G. 'Diapause in Relation to the Ecology of Insects', *Biological Review* (1952)

——, *Introduction to the Study of Animal Populations* (1961)

Atthill, R. *The Somerset & Dorset Railway* (Newton Abbot, 1967)

Avery, B. W. 'The Soils of the Glastonbury District of Somerset', *Soil Survey of Great Britain* (1955)

Bedwell, E. C. 'The County Distribution of the British Hemiptera-Heteroptera', *Entomologists Monthly Magazine*, 81 (1945)

Beirne, B. P. *The Origin and History of the British Fauna* (1952)

——, *British Pyralid and Plume Moths* (1952)

Bertin, L. *Eels* (1956)

Billingsley, J. *View of the Agriculture of Somerset* (1795)

Brinkhurst, R. O. 'The Habits & Distribution of British *Gerris* and *Velia* Species', *Journal of the Society for British Entomology* (1959)

Bristowe, W. S. *The World of Spiders* (1958)

Bulleid, A. and Gray, H. St G. *The Glastonbury Lake Village*, 2 vols (1911, 1917)

——, *The Meare Lake Village* (1953)

Bulleid, A. *The Lake-Villages of Somerset*. The Glastonbury Antiquarian Society (1968)

Butler, A. E. *A Biology of the British Hemiptera Heteroptera* (1923)

Clapham, A. R. and Godwin, H. *Studies of the Post-Glacial History of British Vegetation*—VIII: 'Swamping Surfaces in Peats of the Somerset Levels': IX: 'Prehistoric Trackways in the Somerset Levels', *Trans Philosophical Society* (1948)

Clapham, A. R., Tutin, T. G. and Warburg, E. F. *Flora of the British Isles* (Cambridge, 1958)

Clark, J. A. 'Essay on the Somersetshire Level', *Bath & West of England Agricultural Journal*, 2 (1854)

Clegg, J. *The Freshwater Life of the British Isles* (1952)

Corbet, P. S., Longfield, C. and Moore, N. W. *Dragonflies* (1960)

Cunliffe, B. 'The Somerset Levels in the Roman Period', *Council for British Archaeology Research Report*, 7 (1966)

Dewar, H. S. and Godwin, H. 'Archaeological Discoveries in the Raised Bogs of the Somerset Levels', *Proc Prehistoric Soc* (1963)

Dobson, D. P. *The Archaeology of Somerset* (1931)

Editor. *British Regional Geology—Bristol and Gloucester District*

(HMSO 1935)
Editorial Committee. 'Somerset Birds'. SA & NHS Ornithological Section
Godwin, H. *Studies of the Post-Glacial History of British Vegetation*—VI: 'Correlations in the Somerset Levels', *New Phytologist* (1941)
——, 'Botanical and Geological History of the Somerset Levels', *Advancement of Science*, 12 (1955)
——, *Studies of the Post-Glacial History of British Vegetation*—XIII: 'The Meare Pool Region of the Somerset Levels', *Trans Philosophical Society* (1955)
——, *The History of the British Flora* (Cambridge, 1956)
Gough, J. W. *The Mines of Mendip* (Newton Abbot, 1967)
Greig-Smith, P. *Quantitative Plant Ecology* (1964)
Hadfield, C. *The Canals of South West England* (Newton Abbot, 1967)
Harrison Matthews, L. *British Mammals* (1963)
Hawkins, D. *Sedgemoor and Avalon* (1954)
Helm, P. J. 'The Somerset Levels in the Middle Ages', *Journal of British Archaeology* (1949)
Hendy, E. W. *Somerset Birds* (1943)
Hickin, N. E. *Caddis Larvae* (1967)
Hope-Simpson, J. F., Newton, S. E. and Ricketts, M. J. 'Plant Communities on Shapwick Heath, Somerset', *Proc Bristol Nat Soc* (1963)
Jefferies, R. *Wild Life in a Southern County* (1889)
Kelting, E. L. 'An Outline of the Development of Land Drainage in Somerset', River Board Assoc Annual Conference, Weston-super-Mare (1958)
——, 'The Rivers & Sea Walls of Somerset'. Presidential Address SA & NHS, 1968
Kloet, G. S. and Hincks, W. D. *A Check List of British Insects* (Stockport, 1945)
Lewis, S. *The Breeding Birds of Somerset and Their Eggs* (1955)
Little, B. *Portrait of Somerset* (1969)
Locke, R. 'An Historic Account of the Marshlands of the County of Somerset'. Letters and Papers, Bath & West of England Soc (1796)
——,'Survey of Somerset'. Sevel MS, Taunton Museum (c 1798)
Longfield, C. *The Dragonflies of the British Isles* (1949)
McMahon, A. F. M. *Fishlore* (1946)
Mellanby, H. *Animal Life in Fresh Water* (1938)
Mid-Somerset Naturalist Society, The. Annual Reports (Bridgwater)
Miles, H. and Miles, T. J. *Settlement Sites of the Late Pre-Roman Iron Age in the Somerset Levels*. SA & NHS (1969)
Moss, C. E. *Geographical Distribution of Vegetation in Somerset*. Bath & Bridgwater District Royal Geog Soc (1907)

Murray, R. P. *Somerset County Flora.* SA & NHS (1896)
Neal, E. G. *The Badger* (1948)
—, *The Ecology of the Badger in Somerset.* SA & NHS (1966)
Palmer, E. M. and Ballance, D. K. *The Birds of Somerset* (1968)
Pennington, W. *The History of British Vegetation* (1969)
Perring, F. H. and Walters, S. M. (editors). *Atlas of the British Flora* (1962)
Salisbury, Sir E. *Weeds and Aliens* (1961)
Saunders, E. *The Hemiptera-Heteroptera of the British Isles* (1892)
Savory, T. H. *British Spiders* (Oxford, 1926)
Smith, C. *The Birds of Somersetshire* (1869)
Solomon, M. E. 'Population Dynamics'. Institute of Biology, Study no 18 (1969)
Somerset County Council Planning Dept. *Peat in Central Somerset* (Taunton, 1967)
Somerset County Education Committee. *The Somerset Countryside 1970* (Taunton, 1970)
Southwood, T. R. E. and Leston, D. *Land and Water Bugs of the British Isles* (1959)
Stovin, G. H. T. *The Caterpillars of the British Moths* (1948)
Strasburger, E. *A Text Book of Botany* (1898)
Tansley, A. G. *Britain's Green Mantle* (1949)
—, *The British Isles and Their Vegetation* (Cambridge, 1949)
Tate, W. E. *Somerset Enclosure Acts & Awards.* SA & NHS (1948)
Thomas, C. (editor). *Rural Settlement in Roman Britain.* Council for British Archaeology (1966)
Tucker, B. W. *Notes on Somerset Mammalia.* SA & NHS (1925)
Turner, A. H. *Lepidoptera of Somerset.* SA & NHS (1955)
Vesey-Fitzgerald, B. *The Vanishing Wild Life of Britain* (1970)
Victoria County History. *A History of the County of Somerset* (1906)
Watson, G. A. 'The Water Bugs (Rhyncota-Hemiptera) of North Somerset', *Trans Soc Brit Entomology* (1943)
Watson, W. *The Algae of Somerset,* SA & NHS (1952)
White, G. *The Natural History of Selborne* (1949)
Williams, M. 'Draining Activity in the Somerset Levels since 1939', *Geography* (1964)
—, *The Drainage of the Somerset Levels* (Cambridge 1970)
Witherby, H. F. *et al. The Hand Book of British Birds* (1941)
Willis, A. J. 'The Vegetation of Catcott Heath, Somerset', *Proc Bristol Nat Soc* (1967)
Wilson, W. A. *Coleoptera of Somerset.* SA & NHS (1958)
Yeates, G. K. *Bird Haunts in Southern England* (1947)

Acknowledgements

I would like to acknowledge the help given to me by a large number of people in preparing this book. I am particularly indebted to Mr C. Morris for his drawings and diagrams; to Dr T. T. Macan for his permission to use material which first appeared in the scientific publication of the Freshwater Biological Association; to Mr E. L. Kelting and his staff for making their material available to me and being prepared to spend time in discussion, and to Mr and Mrs L. Morley for their help in preparing the manuscript.

I am also indebted to the friends who have given me encouragement and advice, and particularly to my wife who has borne the brunt of everything, from being walked through marshes to having the house littered with papers and specimens.

Finally I would like to thank the people of Sedgemoor and especially Westonzoyland for their kindness to us, for the information and anecdotes they have related to us and, above all, for making us feel that Sedgemoor is truly our home.

I am grateful to the following for allowing me permission to reproduce illustrations in their possession and for which they hold the copyright. Without their support this new illustrated edition of the book would not have been possible.

Julian Comrie: front and back covers. Douglas Allen: pages 12, 19 (top & bottom), 24, 26, 27, 34, 35, 42, 46, 48, 99 (top & bottom), 110, 128 (bottom), 129 (bottom), 130 (top), 137. Aquarius Studio, Middlezoy: 11, 15 (top & bottom), 51 (top), 59. H. Auger: 116, 117. Dr E. G. Neal: 52, 70, 71, 73, 78, 79, 87, 90, 91, 93, 95 (top & bottom), 105 (bottom), 106, 108, 109 (top & bottom), 114. A. E. Mc. R. Pearce: Frontispiece, 8, 14, 28, 49, 51 (bottom), 62, 63 (top & bottom), 66 (top & bottom), 67, 69, 74 (top & bottom), 77, 80, 89 (top & bottom), 94, 97, 103 (top & bottom), 105 (top), 126 (centre), 131. Colin Poole: 124, 125 (bottom). Somerset County Council, Local History Library: 25. Somerset Rural Life Museum, Glastonbury: 20 (bottom), 29, 32, 41, 47, 124, 126 (top), 127, 128 (top), 129 (bottom), 130 (bottom). The Castle Museum, Taunton: 20 (top), 23. Christopher Willoughby: 102. G. H. E. Young: 113, 115, 118, 119 (top & bottom), 120, 121, 122 (top & bottom), 123.

I would also like to acknowledge the help given by David Lester, Mrs A. H. Napper, and the staff of Wessex Water Authority.

Index